EVALUATING PUBLIC PROGRAMMES:
CONTEXTS AND ISSUES

For Emma Amelia

Evaluating Public Programmes: Contexts and Issues

IAN SHAW
School of Sociology & Social Policy
University of Nottingham

 Routledge
Taylor & Francis Group

LONDON AND NEW YORK

First published 2000 by Ashgate Publishing

Reissued 2018 by Routledge
2 Park Square, Milton Park, Abingdon, Oxon OX14 4RN
711 Third Avenue, New York, NY 10017, USA

Routledge is an imprint of the Taylor & Francis Group, an informa business

A Library of Congress record exists under LC control number: 00134014

ISBN 13: 978-1-138-73965-9 (hbk)
ISBN 13: 978-1-138-73958-1 (pbk)
ISBN 13: 978-1-315-18415-9 (ebk)

Contents

List of Figures

List of Tables and Diagrams

Acknowledgements

Many thanks to Laura Ward-Swietlinska and Linda Poxon who undertook the preparation of the CRC for this work. Thanks also to Ashgate for being understanding of the pressures on my time. I must also thank Ray Pawson who, perhaps inadvertently, introduced me to the sociological approach to evaluation when I replaced his teaching for a year at the University of Leeds back in 1992.

Introduction

When I started out studying public policy as a student I thought that policy formation was based upon sound information and analysis of the impact of policy programmes. I now know that this was somewhat naive and 'the facts' often have little to do with the formulation or the direction of a surprising number of public policies. Those evaluating public policy often find that a significant part of their role is in educating policy makers on the limitation of both their programme and what can be expected from a programme of evaluation research. One could of course argue that public policies have been subject to evaluation for many years. However, such evaluations are often to do with examining costs of a public service frequently in terms of a single criterion: value for money. Such 'evaluations' often focus almost exclusively upon achieving economy savings without exploring how, or even whether the service works. The NHS is perhaps the prime example and many of the case studies in this book refer to that service, though the lessons are wider:

> The major weakness of the National Health Service is that it is not possible to tell whether or not it works. There are no outcome measures to speak of other than that of crude numbers of patients treated. There is little monitoring on behalf of the public. As a result, the correct level of funding for the NHS cannot be determined and the public and politicians cannot decide whether or not they are getting value for the resources pumped into the National Health Service. (Social Services Committee of the House of Commons, 1988, xi)

Because of such misuse of the term, Evaluation has become a misunderstood

1

and often abused term in relation to public programmes. The Collins English Dictionary defines evaluation as 'to find or judge the value of' but, of course, does not explain how this can be achieved. This leads to a wide range of views on what evaluation is and even whether audit or monitoring can be seen as a form of evaluation. This was the subject of a wide ranging discussion on the American Evaluation Association's E-mail discussion list in January of 1998 - only a small section of which is reproduced here.

Richard Duncan argued that:

- The important thing about monitoring and evaluation is that everyone agrees what we mean by the terms we will use in any given evaluation and then we proceed from there.
- The emphasis is on learning.
- Monitoring is - are we doing what we said we were going to do?
- Evaluation is 'so what'.
- Monitoring looks at inputs and outputs.
- Evaluation looks at effects and impacts although there are often overlaps in effects.
- The following characteristics are evident:
  MONITORING
    - keeps track of activities, expenditures, process
    - accepts the policies, rules and conditions which are in place
    - focuses on inputs and outputs
    - tracks implementation
    - concerned with short term accomplishment
    - tries to find out why things are or are not working
  EVALUATION
    - looks at consequences
    - measures objectives
    - questions objectives, policies and procedures in terms of results
    - looks for causes, challenges and unplanned change
    - challenges assumptions
    - seeks lessons learned

Patricia Rogers on the other hand argued that monitoring was more concerned with description than assessment (which is evaluation). Michael Quinn Patton responded that paradigm's have permutations and shifts and the distinction between monitoring and evaluation will often be context based. He went on:

> We're inevitably caught up in attempting to make fine semantic distinctions (e.g. monitoring vs evaluation) that are

2

no less arbitrary and variable. A dispute was reported in today's newspaper in which people are arguing with great passion about the differences between cider (soft not hard) and apple juice. Some perceived them as the same, some as different. Some *experience* them as different some don't. Some want to regulate the supposed differences. You can only call *this* cider (you can only call *this* evaluation). It is critically important to get beyond labels. Monitoring or audit in one setting will be evaluative in its use and intent, and in another will not be. The differences will depend, in part of the perceptions of those involved or the experiences of those involved, or both, or neither.

In my view the difference can be illustrated by way of an analogy. If your goal was to travel from Nottingham to London by car, evaluation would tell you that you had actually arrived and how you got there. Monitoring, on the other hand, can be seen to be a little like navigation as it would ensure that you travelled the right roads and would advise changes in direction if you were not.

Certainly it is the case that the term 'evaluation' has become a part of the modern day apparatus of management and policy making and has become a miss used and misunderstood part of management jargon. In such an environment 'evaluation' can often mean that senior management asks the junior management responsible for the day to day running of the project - 'how's it going?'. To which the junior replies according to how much he or she values their job. One of the aims of this work is to show that evaluation is often far from straightforward and that the theory and practice of evaluation are far from 'fool proof'. There is also a distinction which should be made between evaluation of public policy and evaluation of public programmes. Programmes tend to be the result of policy and, as we shall see, there are different ways of evaluating each.

The work is in a number of chapters. The first chapter outlines the development of evaluation research and highlights the key methodological issues which concern contemporary research. A part of this is the move in emphasis from evaluation concerned with output towards evaluation concerned with understanding 'process' or how programmes work. The chapter concludes by arguing that many of the issues in evaluation research are influenced as much, if not more, by political as they are by methodological considerations. The following chapters build upon this initial argument to examine the issues raised in a number of 'case studies'.

1 The Logic and Development of Evaluation

Causation and Experimental Logic

The epistemological roots of empiricist social research can be traced back at least as far as John Stuart Mill. Put very simply, the nature of empiricist explanation is that the social world is governed by general principles in the same way as the natural world. As a consequence the explanatory strategies of the physical sciences can also be applied to the social world. The method of science, of course, is the experimental approach.

The world, it is argued, is made up of 'entities' (e.g. objects and/or events) and these 'entities' can be the basic unit of social analysis. In sociological explanation a class of objects and/or events are referred to as 'concepts'. As a consequence analysis of the part of the social world we are concerned with should commence by identifying the classes of objects through their observable uniformities. As well as being composed of objects, the universe is also composed of relationships. Two main types of relationship are generally acknowledged in the literature - analytic and synthetic relationships. The world can therefore be analysed by examining objects and their relationship to each other. The difference between analytic and synthetic relationships could be described as a difference between composition and causality.

Analytic relationships are those derived from the composition of the object. It is a part of the objects natural make up. For example, Universities have academics; hospitals have doctors; woodland has trees and so on. Each object may also be broken down into sub categories for analysis. For example Universities can be broken down into old, red-brick, new; doctors can be broken down into

4

junior, consultant, psychiatrist, paediatrician etc; and woodland can be broken down into deciduous, mixed, coniferous etc. These sub-categories are identifiable because they possess a particular range of properties which are readily identifiable.

The synthetic relationship, on the other hand, is concerned with how objects are linked together by chains of events - where object 'A' does something to affect object 'B' etc. The first event acts upon or triggers off the second. An analogy often used is that of the snooker table where the white ball is hit against a coloured ball and drives it into a particular direction. The logic is that the world is composed of an infinite number of these synthetic relationships (like snooker balls crashing into one another). The way to understand the world is explore the sequences of these relationships and discover their regularity.

Types and sub-types of objects can be recognised because of their similar properties. We can also learn the regular sequence of action of these objects upon one another. However, as there are an infinite number of regularities acting simultaneously the world has an appearance of irregularity. This could be because it is difficult to know precisely what regularity is occurring at any particular instance and so the social world is not entirely predictable. As a consequence any particular causal explanation does not work perfectly. If we take, for example the idea that social class determines educational success, this can be refuted by the example of the working class PhD student. The reason why causal relationships do not produce perfect regularities is because there are a number of other regularities also exerting an influence. If the working class PhD student is taken as an example, a number of variables can be identified to account for this phenomena. Variables such as IQ, teachers expectations, type of school etc. All these factors, and more, may also exert an influence. This provides us with a surface appearance of a randomly ordered world where events can be predicted only on probability of occurrence.

However, by use of the scientific method social investigators try to control for the various potential relationships acting upon an object and attempt to establish what the underlying and crucial regularities actually are. This, expressed very crudely, is the basic epistemology and ontology of the approach. The world is perceived to be comprised of objects and types of objects and relationships and types of relationships. As a consequence, evaluators need a methodology which enables the discovery of the causal regularities which are dominant in the part of the world under examination.

The literature on causality is vast and the concept is far from being unproblematic. However, there are broadly two basic schools of thought which will be briefly mentioned here. Harré terms them the generative and successionist schools. The successionist view is that maintained in positivist experimental research and is sometimes called the constant conjecture view. This argues that causes are not real. The world is comprised of objects and causes are not objects. All we can do is infer causality. A causal connection between two events can be inferred because there is a perpetual connection between the two events - that the events occur jointly and that change in one is always accompanied by change in the other. The other important point is that the causal link must be between separate events. This is not to be confused with a relationship of composition where things occur together because they are a part of the same object.

The generative view on the other hand believes that there are real causal mechanisms. This view argues that we are only persuaded that there are causal relationships because we can point to the mechanism which gave rise to the altered state. Here causes do not operate between discrete events but can be perceived as a process which connects two objects. Cause is argued to be a process of internal conversion rather than the successionist view that the two events were acting at a distance.

An examination of the smoking/cancer debate may be of assistance in understanding the difference between these two views of causal relationships. Under a successionist approach the research strategy would attempt to establish the causal link by observing the joint occurrence of the two events - being careful to rule out other potential causes such as diet etc. The generative view on the other hand would argue that it is useless to look at such connections as a link may never be established with any certainty. They argue that the correct approach would be to examine the internal medical chemical and physiological changes that smoking brings about and establish which of those identified is the causal mechanism. Neither of these views believes that correlation proves causation but it is the difference of approach which divides the two views. As a consequence, one way of critically analysing an evaluation is to argue that it operates within an inappropriate view of causality - for example, that a successionist model was adopted when a generative model may have been more appropriate. Evaluations also have a tendency to confuse analytic and synthetic relationships.

The experimental design is the exemplification of the method of causal inference. The principle used is to infer causality. An elaboration of the successionist model provides indicators to causal inference because certain principles about succession are laid down as in figure 1.

However, this does not often provide enough explanation as it does not distinguish spurious regularities from causal ones. Take, as an example, salary and alcohol consumption. If there was an increase in salary and alcohol consumption would this mean that the increased salary actually *caused* the increase in drinking? One would think not. Clearly other causal factors would exist and would need to be taken into account. As a consequence a methodology is required which ensures that the regular conjunction of events is not the result of a conjunction of a range of further processes. Experimental logic provides the foundation of this methodology. A selected group of people are split into two groups - an experimental and control group. This may be done by matching the characteristics (age, sex, education etc.) of the people in the control group as closely as possible with those of the people in the experimental group. Both groups are then observed and /or measured against some ability or other factor in the pre test stage. An independent variable of some sort is then introduced into the

Figure 1: Principles of Succession

Time order: | If **a** causes **b** then **a** occurs before **b**

Association: | Changes in **a** need invariably to be associated with changes in **b** experimental but not the control group. The participants of both groups are then observed and/or measured again. Any difference between the groups is then attributed to the effect of the independent variable. This can be illustrated in table 1.

Unfortunately, many of the variables in public programmes that interest evaluators cannot be manipulated and, as a consequence, this potentially secure method of making causal inferences is not really available. Evaluators in the social world can rarely control a situation so that only one causal influence is acting at a particular time. In the wider world people come under the influence of an infinite number of social factors. Part of the logic, however, can be recovered. Both approaches have identical objectives. Both try to split the world down into variables and examine cause and effect relationships. Often the best the evaluator can do is use a portion of the experimental design - at worst only examining the outcome of independent variables.

In the research of public programmes evaluation is heavily weighted with experimental or scientific connotations. A look at some definitions of evaluation research seem to reinforce this view:

> The use of the *scientific method* to measure the implementation and outcomes of policies and programmes for decision making purposes.
> (Rutman, 1984, p.23)

The other feature which could be added, of course, is what evaluation research is actually for - so Weiss argues:

> The purpose of evaluation research is to measure the effects of a programme against the goals it set out to accomplish as a means of contributing to the subsequent decision making about the programme and improving future programming.
> (Weiss, 1972, p.17)

In essence then, evaluators of public programmes are looking for methods which monitor the implementation of a programme or policy under experimental conditions. As a consequence, some knowledge is required of the variety of experimental strategies and possibilities.

Table 1: Experimental Design

Group	pre-test	cause	effect
Experimental	observation	change	effect observed
Control	observation	---	observation

The Experimental Method

This is all usually explained by setting up the yardstick of the 'ideal' experimental design (see table 1 and figure 2). It is perhaps worthy of note that the 'ideal' is one associated with medical and psychological science - drug testing etc. The logic of experimental design - the classic design - involves the use of pre-test and post-test measurement and also control groups. Control and subject groups are matched against as many characteristics as possible so that they are identical. Consequently the only difference is the application of the intervention (policy or public programme to the experimental and **not** to the control group. A small number of well known examples are considered here in order to illustrate key points:

1. Sesame Street

Sesame Street formed one part of a public programme called 'Operation Head Start'. This was concerned with the notion of pre-schooling. It has long been recognised that people change more between the ages of 2 and 5 than at any other time of our lives. Indeed it was the founder of the Jesuits St. Ignatius of Loyola who first coined the saying:

Give me a child until he is 5 and I will give you the man.

As a consequence one idea in the creation of policies to off-set the educational disadvantage of certain age groups in society, was to start them off in education earlier. Sesame street was a part of the 'head start' package and was aimed at 3 to 5 year olds and supposedly at the disadvantaged (there were black and Hispanic presenters). Two separate field experiments were carried out - with 'kindergarten' and 'at home' groups.

The strategy adopted to evaluate this programme was to target nursery classes in particular areas. These were randomly assigned to groups who were 'encouraged' to view the programme and those who did not view it. The strategy also targeted family homes in the same neighbourhoods - and some were experimental - which basically meant that the parents were canvassed, given publicity material and visited by research staff. The same educational, reading, IQ, and reasoning tests were carried out on all groups (watchers and non-watchers) at the 'before' stage. The programme was ran for a while (months) and then the testing was repeated at the 'after' stage. Those children in the 'watching' group enjoyed some positive results when compared to the 'non-watching' (control) children. The 'watchers' had a tendency to out perform children from equivalent groups. The black watcher out performed the black non-watcher, the middle class watcher tended to out perform the middle class non-watcher. It is perhaps worth mentioning that this evaluation has been repeated since, but the results were not so clear cut as in the original.

9

Figure 2: Evaluation Research Design

The 'classic' experimental design

Stage I

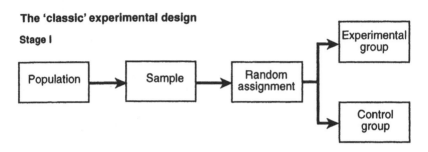

Stage II

	Before	Exposure to policy change	After	
Experimental group	a	Yes	b	If the difference between **b** and **a** is greater than the difference between **d** and **c**, the policy change has had a measurable effect.
Control group	c	No	d	

Quasi-experimental designs

Stage I

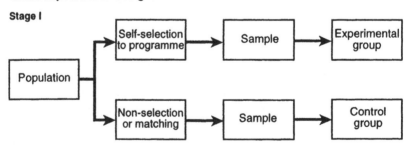

Stage II as above

10

2. The New Jersey Income Maintenance Evaluation

The public policy under scrutiny here is the integrated tax/benefit scheme, also known as the negative income tax scheme. This operates by first dismantling the existing benefit system. Then the taxation system is enlarged so that when people's income falls below a certain level the tax goes the other way - the revenue gives money as opposed to taking it. At not inconsiderable expense [around $8 million on 1968 prices] and with the benefit of a surprisingly imaginative state legislature, the taxation system was changed for a trail period of 4 years - so that some people came under the new negative income tax system and some stayed with the previous tax/welfare system.

The assignment to experimental and control groups was random. However, the results seemed to show that nothing much had changed. For example, there was no change in people's self esteem, health or fertility. However, one of the *non*-changes was seen as important. Many politicians had feared 'labour force withdrawal' as the need to 'sign on' was removed - given that the negative income tax automatically provided monies it was expected to encourage the 'work shy' to be shy. But this did not happen. The only other thing to note about this experiment was that there were in effect eight different experimental groups. Each was set up with a different 'guaranteed income level' and a different rate of tax above that level. Other similar experiments have managed to produce particular results. In Seattle, for example, the divorce rate changed and medical debts reduced, but there was little significant difference.

Before critiquing this approach it is first worth considering the variations on the experimental theme - the quasi experiments.

Discussing Quasi Experimental Evaluations

Quasi-experimental evaluation involve modifications to the 'experimental design' which and are, generally, used more frequently.

Quasi-experimental designs retain some of the basic methods whilst dropping others:

1. The smallest modification retains the before and after quality of the experiment, but just shifts the prior phase involving the allocation of people to groups. In other words the experimental group is *self assigned*. This design encourages people into the two groups (subject and control). Here the strategy admits that often it is the case that one cannot require people to follow a particular programme. As a consequence the basic comparison made is between people who have chosen to do 'something' and people who have not. One can recapture some of the spirit of the experimental process by matching. The aim is to make the two groups as similar as possible by arranging for the same balance of age, sex, education, social class, medical condition - or whatever.

11

Matching, in a design sense is not without weaknesses. Often policies are particularly efficacious for only particular groups in society. Unfortunately one can not always forecast which groups beforehand. As a consequence it is difficult to know which characteristics to match. As an example, if one was evaluating a prison education programme and matching had taken place against social characteristics. It actually may be the case that the programme was particularly effective for a certain class of offenders (in terms of crimes committed) or it might be the length of sentence that was important. It is difficult to forecast such factors.

The one thing that matching cannot adequately control for, of course, is the *motivations* of the people in the two groups. If we imagine comparing a matched group of students, some undergoing education and some not - then clearly the ones choosing the course are self selected, they have engaged in a decision making process. That, in itself, might be the key to success on the course.

2. Another design that perhaps reflects more accurately on the ways that policies really get implemented is the cross-institutional design. This is a design of natural variation. In this instance the strategy accepts that the 'institutions' or 'teams' or 'arrangements' which are put into place to carry out policies will themselves vary. The focus of the evaluation is the measurement of the amount of variation in the 'treatment' and correlate this with the differences in outcomes.

A study by Sinclair and Goldberg (1986) is a good example. This was a study of probation hostels. The evaluators were interested in the abscondence rate and a before and after design was adopted to allow them to examine this rate. They examined the difference in the regime offered - looking at discipline/roles/'warmth'/contact/intake/size/age range and so on, and found that a combination of discipline plus personal contact was the best remedy for preventing premature leaving.

It could be argued that this degree of simplification means that all the logic and validity of the experiment has been lost. As there is no control in the evaluation strategy, nor is there a watch who goes where, it is difficult to know whether the difference in outcomes are due to unknown differences between the clients. Secondly, because the treatment regimes are pre-existing, the evaluator has to rely on guess work and imperfect measures as to what differentiates them.

3. The final design worthy of consideration under this heading (there are others not considered), which bares only the slightest 'family resemblance' to the experiment is the *before and after* study. This is a study of a single project which takes a series of measures of the participants as they go through a programme. For example, if the evaluation was concerned with a training course the strategy would probably include a measure of academic abilities, perceptions, skills etc. before the course commenced (time 1 (pre)) and again when the course ended (time 2 (post)) and supplement these measures by a descriptive/qualitative analysis of the events and process that make up the course. However, few evaluations attempt to match a control group and consequently have lost the comparison yardstick which

is at the heart of the method. Such evaluations have lost any ability to measure the significance of events outside of the course itself which may be changing what you are measuring in people. Evaluators ignore this element at their peril.

Meta-Evaluation: This is another term readers may find in relation to studies of public programmes. This has been defined as the quantitative synthesis of the results of a systematic overview of previous studies. Meta-evaluation consequently is a method of collating and analysing all the available evidence on a particular research question in as systematic a way as possible. The validity of such a quantitative approach will rest upon the method with which the studies have been selected for inclusion in the analysis and the completeness of the evidence collected in the systematic review. In other words the review attempts to gain validity for the process by which it is undertaken. Sackett lists 8 characteristics of systematic review in terms of questions which should be asked of review articles:

- Were the questions and methods clearly stated?
- Were comprehensive search methods used to locate the relevant studies?
- Were explicit methods used to determine which articles were included in the review?
- Was the methodological quality of the primary studies assessed?
- Were the selection and assessment of the primary studies reproducible and free from bias?
- Were the differences in individual study results adequately explained?
- Were the results of the primary studies combined appropriately?
- Were the reviewers conclusions supported by the data cited?

However, the validity of such reviews depends upon obtaining an unbiased estimate of the previous studies conducted in an area. There is now some evidence of both production and citation bias. 'Positive' results are more likely to be published, especially in prestigious journals and are also more likely to be cited by other researchers. There is also pressure from some research funders to publish negative findings. For example in terms of the assessment of new drugs Gotzche concludes:

> Doubtful or invalid statements were found in 76 percent of the conclusions or abstracts. Bias consistently favoured the new drug in 81 trials, and the control in only 1 trial.
> (Gotzche, 1989, pp.31-56)

In other words a meta-analysis can, at best, be only as good as the studies upon which it is based.

Evaluating Experimental Evaluation Research

All of the experimental approaches have common difficulties which will be discussed here. These views have been have been well aired by a number of commentators (cf. Pawson & Tilley, 1997). The experimental design does not have the power to wholly convince which it once enjoyed and this is largely because the results have been, on balance, inconclusive. As will be discussed later this was a major issue as it led in turn to a 'nothing works' view of public policy. Having made such comment, the criticisms made here are not intended as a condemnation of the approach - rather a critique to aid good practice.

Unclear Goals

Alice's conversation with the Cheshire Cat in Wonderland is useful to illustrate the difficulty of trying to achieve something with unclear goals:

> 'Would you tell me, please, which way I aught to go from here?'
> 'That depends a great deal upon where you want to get to', said the Cat.
> 'I don't much care where', said Alice.
> 'Then it doesn't matter which way you go', said the Cat.
> 'So long as I get somewhere', Alice added as an explanation.
> 'Oh, you are sure to do that', said the Cat, 'if only you walk long enough'.

It is obvious that if you don't know where you want to go, then you'll have trouble getting there and what is worse, you will not know when you've arrived! Unclear goals or objectives imply just this kind of lack of clarity. Of course evaluations sometimes begin without defining goals clearly beforehand in order to avoid the problem of 'goal wars' between competing sets of stakeholder interests. In one example, from skiing, instructors are asked to ensure that a general aim includes 'SMARTER' goals towards those aims:

Specific
Measurable
Agreed
Realistic
Time phased
Exciting
Recorded

It could be argued that the same should apply for public organisations. One of the exercises I use with students is perhaps worth mentioning here in order to illustrate the argument. I supply them all with a piece of sticky 'post it' paper and ask them, without conferring, to write down the most important thing about the room. I then ask them to stick all the pieces of paper on one wall and ask them to examine them and to reflect upon the exercise. Although some students may concur in their observations the majority, of course, do not. This reinforces the point that one must have some criteria for observation, some hypothesis to test, in order to know what is important in advance. This provides a state purposed purpose for an evaluation which gives clear direction. This enables evaluators to be trained to look for the same thing. Of course there may be a conflict over which criteria (or even hypothesis) to adopt. This is influenced by the pressures of stakeholders and will be discussed later in this work.

Evaluation basically compares inputs and outputs. To do this one needs a very clear expression of the intended outcomes of the programme. It must, of course, be recognised that policies are often formulated much more in the context of political discourse than with an eye on measurable outcomes. The consequence of this is that researchers often find themselves trying to satisfy a wide range of interests and this may result in the inclusion of many variables and measures in an arbitrary way in order to see what comes out of it. This reality is worth examining in the context of one of the previous examples.

Take the example of Prison Research. Evaluating the impact of University level education in the prison context. The project (at a prison in Yorkshire, UK) was set without any explicit set of objectives, aspirations, hypotheses other than in broad terms to see if it is feasible - to see how it would be beneficial. So the researchers began with the task of trying to find out what it was they were trying to research. They asked the Home office/ teaching staff/ inmates etc. - what they wanted from the programme and got a disparate list of responses. Some of these involved *psychological* readings, some *moral* readings some *practical* etc. So the research, far from being focussed, was trying to chase after an impossible number of ends. However, unclear goals do not constitute the essential drawback of the method. It is possible to be quite explicit about the aims of a programme. This does not often happen in practice, but it could be achieved. Much the same could be said about other criticisms. The real drawback of the method has to do with context.

Examples in real experiments in psychology labs where there is an experimental and control group split - where the control group literally does nothing and the stimulus is put to the experimental group. Researchers here can be fairly safe in assuming that the experimental stimulus is the only difference between the groups. However, this does not apply to experimental strategies applied in the wider society. Consider *Sesame Street*. One group 'views' the programme and one does not. What does *viewing* the programme actually mean? Viewing takes place over a number of weeks, there is accordingly the variable - **intensity** of viewing. The researcher does not actually sit over and watch the children point their faces at the television. Secondly, staff went to encourage and discuss the watching with the children and parents. Clearly staff were different and

15

the levels of discussion different. Consider now the control groups - they were not prevented from watching - they were not encouraged *not* to watch and they were *not* followed up. So it may be the case that many of them will have actually watched *Sesame Street*. So it is not possible to achieve perfect levels of control in the field.

In medical research or psychological research the experimental/independent variable is a single stimulus - a drug/ treatment/ condition - a variable. In field experimentation concerning public policy the independent variable is a programme. Any programme will contain an infinite number of factors. Consider again the *Sesame Street* TV programmes and the trained staff which encourage participation. Consider the education programme in prison - What is involved in the programme?. The subject matter, the content, the lecturers, classroom interaction, personality of the group, physical setting etc. There are literally scores of factors which could be influential in bringing about change. Moreover, different factors could influence different members of the group. What could be influential in changing one person would not necessarily mean a thing to someone in a slightly different position. This really leaves policy evaluators with two choices. The experimental approach could be abandoned altogether or there must be significant investigation into the processes involved in programmes.

Summarising the Weakness of the Experimental Approach

Public policies and programmes are not 'variables' but complex social processes. A welfare/taxation policy, for example, will involve everything from political beliefs about the role of the state, assumptions about human nature with regard the work ethic, to concerns about where taxation should be in relation to poverty lines. In addition there are all the working practicalities about how to run and administer the scheme - and millions of other points besides.

It is here that the central strategy of experimental research is deficient. Even if one did manage to compare a situation with a programme and then compare it to one where it is absent, it would still not be possible to identify what processes have been responsible for the change and how. As Pawson and Tilley recently pointed out (1997) this is the key reason why follow up and replicate studies are often inconsistent. To actually install a social programme into an institution - one is in effect applying a set of ideas to a context. As a consequence the working of the programme is effected by the practicalities and relative power of the persons implementing, researching and funding it - and this will vary from context to context. Experimentation requires that the context is irrelevant, that it is stripped away. However, it is the different contexts which changes and alters meanings. It therefore follows that evaluation research must get into the process of policy formulation and programme delivery. This is widely recognised, and is the reason why much of contemporary evaluation research declares itself to be concerned with *process* rather than *outcome*.

16

Process Evaluation

Within this broad strategy of process evaluation it is possible to detect many variations. However four main variations will be considered here.

- Constructivism
- Theory Driven Evaluation
- Intervening Variable Evaluation
- Impact Evaluation

There are many more sub-divisions and overlaps on these variations (such as causative probing and intended and unintended outcome analysis) but these four basic approaches form the substantive core of this strategy.

One of the best known works in Constructivism is the approach highlighted in the work of Guba and Lincoln's *4th Generation Evaluation*. However, this work is problematic not least because its critique is of a dated form of positivism which even the positivist's have moved away from. They seem convinced that the current idea in positivism is that there exists some single true realism, driven by natural laws which are open to discovery and harnessing by the methods of science. Also, this work is entirely a programmatic statement. It does not give any examples of how the evaluation (or what they term the 'constructivist method') will work in practice.

However, the approach is worth consideration because it has claimed some success in some contexts and it also demonstrates how the concept of evaluation can become transformed by an adherence to the principles of interpretive social science. In this approach evaluation becomes *negotiation*. The starting point is that the parameters of an evaluation are normally set by clients/sponsors or (if as normal) these are not crystal clear then the client and evaluator between them will establish what the goals of an inquiry are. The constructivist approach discards this and instead adopts a strategy of responsive focussing. This involves identification of all of the stakeholders. A 'stakeholder' is anyone for whom the policy or programme has consequences, and the aim is to build the focus of the research upon conceptual purity. They list 14 main types and subtypes of stakeholder. The stakeholders typically consist of those who implement the policy and those who receive it.

The evaluation itself consists of the evaluators being a kind of negotiator who collects together the constructions of each group's claims, concerns and issues. They then put each groups constructions to the other groups and see if any joint construction can in fact emerge (see figure 3). The unresolved claims they then put to a final big negotiation.

The way in which this approach identifies shortfalls in standard evaluation studies is important. It is very hard to deny that the recipients views on what is happening or supposed to be happening is rather crucial (to put it mildly) to the 'success', or otherwise, of a policy. The approach also points to an interesting

Figure 3: The Flow of Fourth Generation Evaluation

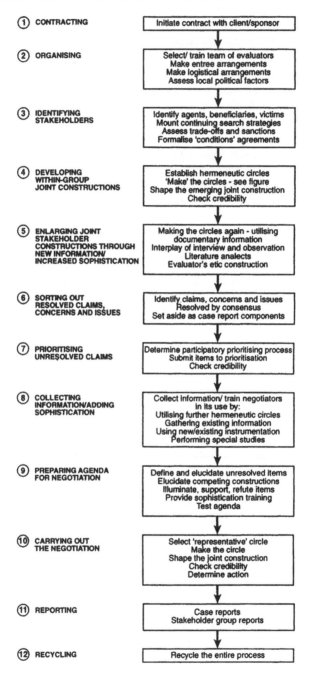

① CONTRACTING	Initiate contract with client/sponsor	
② ORGANISING	Select/ train team of evaluators Make entree arrangements Make logistical arrangements Assess local political factors	
③ IDENTIFYING STAKEHOLDERS	Identify agents, beneficiaries, victims Mount continuing search strategies Assess trade-offs and sanctions Formalise 'conditions' agreements	
④ DEVELOPING WITHIN-GROUP JOINT CONSTRUCTIONS	Establish hermeneutic circles 'Make' the circles - see figure Shape the emerging joint construction Check credibility	
⑤ ENLARGING JOINT STAKEHOLDER CONSTRUCTIONS THROUGH NEW INFORMATION/ INCREASED SOPHISTICATION	Making the circles again - utilising documentary information Interplay of interview and observation Literature analects Evaluator's etic construction	
⑥ SORTING OUT RESOLVED CLAIMS, CONCERNS AND ISSUES	Identify claims, concerns and issues Resolved by consensus Set aside as case report components	
⑦ PRIORITISING UNRESOLVED CLAIMS	Determine participatory prioritising process Submit items to prioritisation Check credibility	
⑧ COLLECTING INFORMATION/ADDING SOPHISTICATION	Collect information/ train negotiators in its use by: Utilising further hermeneutic circles Gathering existing information Using new/existing instrumentation Performing special studies	
⑨ PREPARING AGENDA FOR NEGOTIATION	Define and elucidate unresolved items Elucidate competing constructions Illuminate, support, refute items Provide sophistication training Test agenda	
⑩ CARRYING OUT THE NEGOTIATION	Select 'representative' circle Make the circle Shape the joint construction Check credibility Determine action	
⑪ REPORTING	Case reports Stakeholder group reports	
⑫ RECYCLING	Recycle the entire process	

18

facilitating role for the evaluator by pointing out that the respective articulateness of the parties will differ. One role of the evaluator might well be as a translator. For example, a parent talks about the 'rough end of the stick' that their young child is getting at school - although expressed in terms of the child and the teacher - may actually be about some pedagogic construction.

Less credibly there are some obvious problems with this approach (Pawson, 1996; Pawson & Tilley, 1997). The most interesting claim of this approach is also perhaps the most doubtful. This approach changes the criteria of success in evaluation. This has been termed the 'constructivist three-step' by Pawson (1996) where the strategy is to:

> 1. *Seek out the subject.* Abandoned is any notion that social initiatives can be understood as 'independent variables'. Rather, they are regarded as complex processes of understanding and interaction. Whatever the program, in whatever circumstances, it will 'work' through a process of reasoning change influence, negotiation, battle of wills, persuasion, arbitration or some such like. Evaluation thus has the task of capturing the knowledgeable subject in the act of producing change and this invariably involves the use of some suitable first hand empathetic field methodology such as ethnography.
>
> 2. *Size up the stakeholders.* This emphasis on the actor's point of view tends to have gone hand in hand with a rather more sensitive outlook on the number of influential players in a program. Thus, whilst experimentalists might only have eyes for experimental and control groups, and auditors would look to policy makers and pay masters, constructivists attempt to accommodate stakeholders by the dozen. Guba and Lincoln (1989), for instance, differentiate between 'agents', 'beneficiaries' and 'victims', each category itself being subdivided to number 14 in all. Fieldwork thus has the additional task of searching for points of collective understanding, misunderstanding and potential understanding between the various pockets.
>
> 3. *Parley with participants.* This is the stage with the greatest practical variation, but the basic idea is to push to a more genuinely collective understanding of an initiative. The social world is fundamentally a process of negotiation; so are programs - and so, therefore, should be the research act. In Guba and Lincoln's hands this amounts to providing a sort of arbitration, conciliation and evaluation service. By stages, they recommend that the researcher deciphers the standpoints of each group of stakeholders, generates shared understandings

by twos and threes by way of 'joint constructions', and presses to further enlarge consensus within 'hermeneutic dialectic circles'.
(Pawson, 1996, p.214)

In this approach the success of a programme is not defined in terms of outcomes - changing policies in the way that clients and providers want them to change - but in terms of establishing a match between the constructions of all the stakeholder. This provides a major difficulty. In anything other than an immediate small-scale issue of policy it is very difficult to contemplate what this final 'joint construction' would look like. The reason is that (in the UK at least) disparity is the norm throughout society's organisations and there seems little reason to believe that providing this vehicle for exchange of views will bring them together. What is more, Ethnographers are now less certain whether their efforts end up 'reproducing' or 'constructing' reality (Hammersley, 1992). Perhaps most important is that the 'conceptual parity' the method seeks is not particularly feasible in the face of *lack* of parity in terms of power, politics, knowledge etc. For example, is it possible to incorporate all the conflicting demands in an agreed welfare/ taxation system? Parliaments have been thrashing this out for a hundred years and things do not seem to have arrived at a joint construction.

As will be discussed later, confronting different perspectives is an implicit and unrecognised aspect of an evaluation. For instance, there may be some members of the staff in secure mental hospitals who work within the expectation that therapeutic communities involves a 'psychological defects' model. Over time they may be possibly persuaded to a majority view that it is really about providing alternative perspectives etc. However, if you move to another group of stakeholders - prison officers - one would be faced with an enormous variety of views within the ranks - welfare centred views; custodial views etc. Perhaps the majority may even consider that Therapeutic Communities have no role to play at all! It is quite inconceivable that such a gap could be closed by creating hermeneutic circles.

Guba and Lincoln's model for applied qualitative research is at one end of the spectrum in that it searches for a radically new strategy. Most claims for the qualitative style of evaluation are rather less grand, often doing little more than emphasising that the qualitative method gains more information on the workings of society. Two good examples of this are work by Finch and Smith respectively. They, separately, discuss the importance of looking at the recipient of the programmes and in examining the unintended outcomes of policy making. Finch's study was of pre-school play groups in deprived working class areas. These were promoted by the council but basically ran on a self help basis. Finch (1983) found an enormous commitment to the idea, but also a failure to sustain it. The policy encouraged women to take an inherently middle class model which they had neither the economic nor the cultural reserves to sustain. She argues that she was able to chart this huge ambivalence which could not have been detected by any other means.

Smith's (1995) example is of a day hospital service for confused elderly patients and in particular the function of the 'relatives group' which was supposed to serve as a forum for people to share their problems and to help coordinate activities between hospital and home. What they found was that while the group served many positive functions it also began to serve, over time, some quite unintended functions. One of these functions, for the hospital, was to cope with meddlesome relatives in this setting, which kept them off the backs of staff elsewhere. At the meetings staff made suggestions in general terms about, say, diet and many relatives came away not knowing whether the advice was 'in general' or really about their 'mum or dad'. Another finding was that the staff were able to control requests for 'special arrangements' (i.e. attending one day less, or more occasionally) by generally erecting the notion that large numbers of people were waiting for places.

Such arguments are possibly undeniable. Ethnography is the best method available for collecting rich, detailed and useful information. However, that is not the problem. The problem with ethnography is in putting the material together.

> Certain contemporary, narratively oriented schools of ethnography adopt the customary starting point that all human action is meaningful, that all beliefs are constructions, but adds the twist that we cannot, therefore, get beyond constructions. In other words, they insist that there are no neutral/factual/definitive accounts to be made of a socially negotiated social world. Every claim, description or explanation about social life carries with it the assumption of the individual making the claim, description or explanation.. we can say of any prolonged period of field observation, or any cycle of evaluation negotiations, that they will generate thousands of separate thoughts and actions which are open to an infinitive number of descriptions. The researchers account of such an open-ended reality must therefore be selective and rests upon his of her preferred assumptions, pet theories, cherished values, and so on. Since on this view there is no single objective reality to report upon, hermeneutic dialectic circles (not surprisingly) go round in circles, rather than constituting a linear advance on the 'truth'.
> (Pawson, 1996, p.216)

As only a fragment of the field research gets reported there is little in the method to prevent the researcher selecting from the study that which he or she wants the report to tell. Since in the 'applied' area there is often an even more direct line to political practice than in the pure area. Applied ethnography lives under the cloud of political bias. The ethnographers usual reaction to this claim is to argue that such an argument could also be applied to quantitative researchers, and that politicians are often overly impressed by numbers. This is probably true, but does not deflect from the central argument. As a consequence, applied ethnographers are faced with exactly the same dilemma of deciding whether their efforts are just subjective viewpoints in a world of subjectivities - or whether there is some grounding in method which gives them some demonstrable warrant. Ethnographers, following the latter route, stress two analytic strategies whereby they accumulate evidence into a model. These are analytic induction and pattern explanation.

Analytic induction, expressed simply, consists of the following stages: A rough estimation and a hypothetical explanation is made of the phenomenon to be explained; Cases are studied in the light of this hypothesis, with the aim of testing whether the hypothesis fits the facts of each particular case; if the hypothesis does not fit, then it is reformulated or the phenomena is redefined so that discrepant cases are not included; the cycle is then repeated with the emphasis on seeking cases to disprove the hypothesis. An example of the use of analytic induction is Lindesmith's study of opium addicts and addiction (1947). In pattern explanation any claim, behaviour or social theme is explained by specifying its place within an identified pattern. This is hard to express formally, but the finished research should convey the feeling that there are no 'loose ends' and that some overall pattern has emerged within which the phenomenon can be described and explained. An example of the use of this strategy is Becker's study of medical students 'Boys in White' which identified an explanatory system and the phenomenon was analysed by locating events within that system.

Internet debate: The value of outcome evaluation and the search for performance indicators forms a topic of continued debate in the evaluation community. On one of the main evaluation discussion lists (Goveteval) during October of 1996 this topic formed the focus of an interesting debate. The key arguments are reflected below. Discussion was initiated by Paul Bullen who wrote the following message to the list:

> It is theoretically impossible in human services to have performance indicators to measure outcomes that can be used at the judge of services (because of the nature of complex systems, the openness of human service systems, lack of control, difficulty of showing cause and effect, the individuality of those receiving services etc, etc. And yet many people want to do just this. The notion of having a few performance indicators to be the measure of outcomes and judge of human services has intrinsic appeal even though it is theoretically impossible.

Bullen then went on to postulate as to why there should be an intrinsic appeal in quantification. He writes:

> We are human and we love to have things in order...; we like to know that we are doing a good job and find it very difficult to be in a position when we have to admit that we don't know whether or not we are doing a good job; Governments need to be able to say they are doing a good job and generate simple information to use in debate. While I know this is true what I don't understand is why politicians always know that any set of numbers (e.g. the unemployment rate) is open to two different interpretations and is publicly debated when released, but within government departments there is an expectation of developing numbers that aught to be beyond debate and speak for themselves; We are able to hold contradictions within us, so for example we can collect a few numbers to measure outcomes because the Director General of the Department says so and at the same time know that we are in a complex world and by and large the numbers are meaningless but we collect them anyway.

This line of argument was subject to quick reaction by Michael Scriven who replied:

> Maybe you should start by sharing with us your grounds for thinking performance indicators are 'theoretically impossible'. I assume you accept that practical evaluation is willing to tolerate *some slippage* between indicators and the true state of affairs for which they are to serve as indicators.

Bullen responded with reflexivity;

> I would be most interested if someone would present grounds for thinking that performance indicators are 'theoretically possible!'. Guy Peters (1989) *The Politics of Bureaucracy* (3rd ed.), Longman, New York wrote: 'A problem that besets MBO, PBBS, or any system attempting to install "rational" policy analysis in government is that operational indicators of the attainment of objectives must be developed in order for the system of performance evaluation to be effective. Unfortunately, the search for such indicators rivals the search for the philosophers stone in its apparent futility.' (p.49.) This is **not** a theoretical argument against performance indicators; it is a claim made by someone with some experience and

expertise... I may have missed it, but in my reading I have yet to find a theoretical basis for believing in the *general* utility of performance indicators in the context of program evaluation... if we don't have a logical argument that shows why or how performance indicators should be used, why should we be surprised if they don't always work.

This was responded to by a number of contributors, but Jerome Winston's is particularly worthy of note. He argued that although there are many sources for the intrinsic appeal of performance indicators including the point that indicators *are* actually perceived to work very well in every day life:

a) My doctor monitors a range of 'vital signs' as indicators of my state of 'health'. My blood pressure goes above x/y and my cholesterol level goes above z: my doctor is concerned. Why? These are not direct measures of health, but high values have been shown to be good *predictors* of conditions that I wish to avoid.

b) The cloud pattern in the sky indicates to me that it is likely to rain, so I take my raincoat c) My partner looks at me in a 'certain way' (indicator) and I draw certain conclusions (which although not always correct are sufficiently often correct for me to use the look as an 'indicator').

In other words, there is intrinsic appeal for 'indicators' because people experience that they often work in day to day life. They may not remember the many times that indicators fail.

It was Ian Davies, The Auditor General of British Columbia, Canada, who attempted to 'square the circle' and reconcile the two approaches:

To someone with a hammer everything looks like a nail. Performance indicators are signs that help define and provide information about the performance construct. They are tools to facilitate measurement and assist us in forming judgement about performance.

Paul Bullen's theoretical impossibility appears to me to refer to at least two things: first, that it is likely misguided to equate a construct with the sum of its indicators, no matter how good these indicators might be in terms of their construct validity; and second, that it is likely just as misguided to attempt to tackle the methodological challenges of outcome attribution by manipulating indicators. From my own practical experience in the public sector, problems with indicators arise more from

24

ways in which the information they provide is improperly used, rather than because of the intrinsic properties of the indicators.

In my mind, accountability for performance indicators, means showing that the program is being managed by keeping ones eye on the outcome ball, rather than focussing solely on process factors. To do this usually requires that the program have identified some indicators of outcome to help it obtain some information about the relevance of the programme. This information should help the program make decisions about its performance, and explain to stakeholders how and why decisions were made.

Goal displacement is usually a defensive reaction to the misuse of performance paraphernalia. To my knowledge the only way to get around this is to get buy-in from the program by, among other things, involving it in generating performance information that is meaningful and helpful to all the program stakeholders.

These extracts from a lively debate illustrate just some of the arguments concerning the value of quantitative approaches to evaluation. The point of clarification which I made to the debate is that performance indicators and outcome measures do not actually *measure* outcome. They are instead *indicators* of what an outcome or performance may actually be. The distinction made by Ian Davies between concept and indicator is important here. Unemployment measures, for example, do not actually *measure* unemployment - all they can do is provide an indication of what the concept (the level of unemployment) may look like. The reliability of indicators vary and can usually only be judged with reference to another indicator. If the two separate indicators discover similar results then the validity of both indicators is strengthened (not proven). If they differ then a value judgement has to be made about which is likely to be most representative of the construct. Because of the desirability of multiple indicators evaluators often mix methodologies, often in triangulation, in order to increase the 'worth' of their research. If they also mix paradigms and include qualitative as well as quantitative methods then they are able to deflect at least some criticism from each 'camp'.

Patton has identified one means of achieving methodological mixes:

The first is through triangulation of methodologies in the study of the same phenomena or programme. In the case of evaluation research this can mean using both quantitative and qualitative strategies to study the same programme.
(Patton, 1980, p.109)

25

The concept of triangulation is based upon work by Denzin (1978). Denzin identified four basic types of triangulation:

1.   Data triangulation: the use of a variety of date sources in a study.
2.   Investigator triangulation: the use of several different research workers or evaluators.
3.   Theory triangulation - the use of more than one theory in the study of a problem or programme.
4.   Methodological triangulation - the use of multiple methods to study a single problem of programme.

As figure 4 shows, methodological mixing can also include theory triangulation as two different methodological paradigms are involved - the holistic-inductive and the hypothetical-deductive.

Denzin explains that the logic of triangulation is based upon the premise that:

> ...no single method ever adequately solves the problem of rival causal factors... because each method reveals different aspects of empirical reality. Multiple methods of observation must be employed. This is termed triangulation. I now offer as a final methodological rule the principle that multiple methods should be used in every investigation.
> (Denzin, 1978, p.28)

Patton supports Denzin's principle and affirms that:

> Triangulation is ideal (and) ... to be highly recommended. Indeed the capability to implement a strategy of triangulation means that evaluators must include in their repertoire of skills the ability to use qualitative methods.
> (Patton, 1980, p.109)

However, Patton goes on to argue that while triangulation is ideal, it is not always possible for a number of reasons. Patton's alternative approach to achieving methodological heterogeneity is:

> ...to borrow and combine parts from pure methodological strategies. To accomplish this it is necessary to separate the measurement, design and analysis components of the hypothetico-deductive and the holistic-inductive paradigms... mixing measurement, design and analysis.
> (Patton, 1980, p.109)

Figure 4: Mixing Paradigms

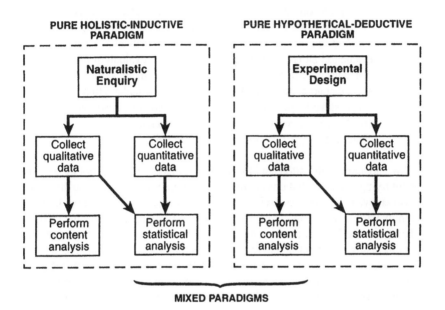

It is because of these approaches that Patton argues evaluation becomes separated from research. Research, Patton maintains, is aimed at 'truth' whilst evaluation should be aimed at 'action' - i.e. the production of information meant to affect policy-making and improve programme effectiveness.

Moreover, Patton argues that an evaluation is not 'repeatable' and should not be regarded a scientific in that sense.

> The philosophical perspective that under grids creative evaluation is the recognition that *there is no one best way to conduct an evaluation*. This insight is critical... Every evaluation situation is unique. A successful evaluation (one that is useful, practical, ethical and accurate) emerges from the special characteristics and conditions of a particular situation - a mixture of people, politics, history, context, resources, constraints, values, needs, interests and chance.
> (Patton, 1980, p.110 - emphasis in original)

I would agree with Patton, and I would argue that evaluation is not *necessarily* about trying to ensure that ones findings are generalisable. This is the difference between evaluation and research, in my mind is that evaluation is about trying to identify what makes programmes or policies work. As we shall see this involves identifying the key factors in a programme's success (or otherwise) and then hypothesising or predicting how those factors may vary from context to context. This means that evaluators should attempt to establish how generalisable the importance of the mechanisms are - not the outcome findings themselves. Put simple, quantitative research seeks 'truth' and evaluation may utilise quantitative research to seek understanding. The reasoning for this argument is presented through the various following sections.

Theory Driven Evaluation: this is another mainstream evaluation method that claims to deal with process rather than outcomes. This is a very important method for evaluation of public programmes and this work will examine the theory in a little more detail than that of the preceding strategies. The basic concept is that what is evaluated is the theories about programme, held by the various stakeholders, rather than the programmes themselves. This could be argued to be a means of substituting for the lack of clear organisational goals.

The concept of theory driven evaluation is not new, for example Suchman in his book Evaluation Research, back in 1967, refers to the importance of what he termed programme theories. However, it was Weiss (1972) who first seriously argued for the basing of evaluation around the theories held about a programme. This work also contained a figure illustrating a number of different theories on which a teacher's home visiting might be based. This is reproduced here to aid explanation (figure 5).

Although a number of authors subsequently explored the concept of evaluating on the basis of a programmes theories it was not until 1990 that another key work

Figure 5: Theory of a Programme of Teacher Home Visits

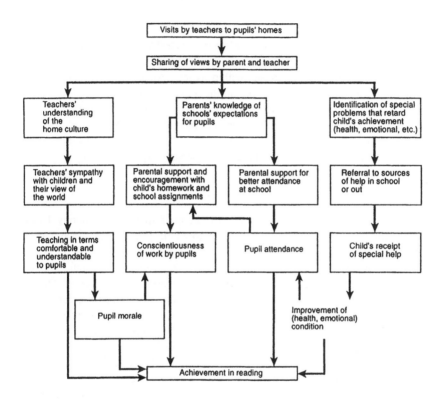

Source: Carol H. Weiss, Evaluation Research. Englewood Cliffs, NJ: Prentice-Hall, 1972, p. 50

was to develop with Huey-Tsyh Chen's *Theory Driven Evaluation*. Chen distinguished between normative and causal theory and argued that evaluation should not be concerned with 'ad-hoc' hypotheses but with social science theories. Chen argued that normative theory 'provides guidance on what goals and outcomes should be pursued or examined' (Chen, 1990, p.43) whereas causal theory consisted of a set of assumptions about how the programme works. As Weiss argues:

> If evaluation can show the series of micro-steps that lead from inputs to outcomes, then causal attribution *for all practical purposes* seems to be within reach. Although such an evaluation can not rule out all the threats to validity we have come to know and love, it has the advantage (if things go well) of showing what processes lead to the outcomes observed; if some of the posited steps are not borne out by the data, then the study can show where the expected sequence of steps breaks down.
> (Weiss, 1996, p.3)

Weiss goes on to argue that this would hold true in community based programmes, when random assignment is impossible, as it does in 'place- based' programmes. There are a number of studies now reported which have traced the emergence of steps in the programme theory. These range from simple to more complex theories: e.g. Sheard *et al.* (1976) examined the use of lithium administered to aggressive prisoners. The evaluation examined the number of violent episodes each committed. The evaluation tested the simple theory that lithium would reduce violence. Cohen and Rice (1995) on the other hand utilised more complex theories in their examination of the effects of involving parents in prevention of adolescent substance abuse. They found parents difficult to engage and infrequent attenders to the programme. What is more many did not believe their children's friends also used drugs and so did not monitor their peer group interactions.

In a recent survey by Weiss (1996) the conditions conducive to theory based evaluation were explored. One of these was theory-based programme planning. Two areas which use this planning approach fairly extensively is risk prevention/management and health promotion. For example, a fairly common theory underlining health promotion programs is social learning theory. The program provides information (for example on how to stop smoking) which leads to a change in motivation and intention (willingness to reduce smoking) which leads to change in practice (cessation of smoking). In addition social-reinforcement theory may call for provision of social support to encourage and sustain smoking cessation. The evaluation should trace the anticipated sequence of changes over time.

30

Chen (1990) argues that both the experimental and the ethnographic approaches tend to treat programmes as having an independent existence. They look at what programmes do to the clients from different points of view - but assume that the programmes are somehow given. The argument is that the research method used follows from the theory under test. What follows is that there is no prescribed method. Simple theories, like normative theory, produces a method which may be close to the standard quasi-experimental approach. However, the more composite the theories are the less-standard and more complex becomes the methodology.

As theory based evaluation has gained both credibility and use over time, confusion has also developed over understanding of the concept. Different varieties of recommended evaluation strategies may all claim to be 'theory based' evaluation. Weiss (1996) attempts to distinguish between these various strategies by making a distinction between what she terms 'program theory' and 'implementation theory'. Weiss argues that programmatic theory deal with the *mechanisms* that intervene between the delivery of a service and the occurrence of outcomes. The mechanisms are not the programme activities themselves but the responses which the programme generates. Weiss uses the example of a contraceptive counselling programme to clarify the issues:

> If contraceptive counselling is associated with reduction in pregnancy, the cause of change might seem to be the counselling. But the mechanism isn't the counselling (the program activity) but the programme process. A common assumption would be that the mechanism is the knowledge that the counselling provides. But knowledge might not be the operative mechanism. It might be that the existence of the counselling program helps to overcome cultural taboos against family planning; it might give women confidence and bolster their assertiveness in sexual relationships; it might trigger a shift in the power relation between men and women. These or any of several other cognitive/affective/social responses would be the mechanisms leading to the desired outcomes.
> (Weiss, 1996, p.9)

Weiss also distinguishes the above from implementation theory which deals with how the programme is carried out. The theoretical assumption this tests is that if the programme is conducted as planned, then the desired results will occur. Weiss argues that this does not really amount to theory based evaluation. She cites the work of McGraw (1996) by means of example: McGraw evaluated a programme to change student's dietary knowledge and food choices in order to reduce the risk of cardiovascular disease in later life. The program, called CATCH (Child and Adolescent Trial for Cardiovascular Health) contained several components. The outcomes studied were the children's dietary knowledge, confidence in being able to select healthier foods and intentions to eat more wisely. These were analysed against input variables (student, teacher and information characteristics) as well as programme processes. The analysis concluded with information on the extent to which programme activities (as defined by the CATCH planners) led to reduced risk and intended preventative behaviour (healthy eating). Although this study makes good use of process measures in analysis of outcomes Weiss argues it does not provide a test of programmatic theory. The theory underlying the programme is described as 'modification of psycho social factors... leading to changes in risk-factor behaviours' (McGraw *et al.*, 1996, p.292). Weiss argues the evaluation did not address the modification of psycho-social factors in that it did not explore the mechanisms by which change is brought about.

The difference between programme theory and implementation theory is analogous to the distinction between mediator and moderator variables discussed by Baron and Kenny (1986). These are both third variables that affect the relationship between independent and dependent variables. The moderator variable is a characteristic, such as gender or frequency of exposure, whose components may have different relations to the outcome variable (e.g. those who attend the programme regularly will do better than those who do not). On the other hand a mediator variable '...represents the generative mechanism through which the focal independent variable is able to influence the dependent variable of interest' (Baron & Kenny, 1986, p.173). In other words the moderator helps to explain which features of people or situations have the highest relationship to the outcome whereas mediators help to explain how the process works. Of course most programmes will contain both kinds of theories and Weiss terms evaluations which explore both equally 'theories of change' evaluations.

Chen handles this 'confusion' as to what constitutes theory based evaluation theory slightly differently. He cites a large number of cases in a sort of typology and some of these are worth examining briefly here.

Normative treatment evaluation: Put simply all this means is that the treatment/ programme or policy under review needs to be properly specified. For evaluation to take place it is important to know precisely what is being evaluated. This would seem to be obvious, but Chen argues that many programmes start with unclear aims and consequently a gap appears between aims and implementation. Another is *Implementation environment evaluation*. This consists of another call for operational clarity. Chen argues that it is important to specify in advance the target groups for whom policy or programme is supposed to work. Policies are generally aimed at quite broad groups - for example; the poor, the disabled, the elderly and so forth. What often happens is that the policies do not work uniformly for the population as a whole but are particularly advantageous for particular sections or groups within the programme. These are often people who are socially better placed to benefit from the programme.

Chen argues that the context and environment aught to be specified in advance of the evaluation because it forces the evaluator and stakeholders to *why* the programme works. Chen provides a number of interesting case studies. One is the

32

feature of a programme to implement an educational information pack about mental illness in a remote Canadian community. The concept was that it would smooth the way towards a community care approach to the release of psychiatric patients. The supposition behind the programme was that fear, rooted in ignorance, was the problem to be overcome within the communities. As a consequence, education was aimed at providing more knowledge of the causes and consequences of mental illness. The programme was evaluated by a typical before/after control group study which found little change in attitudes towards the mentally ill. The reason was that this was a strong 'law and order' community and they preserved order by shunning and protecting themselves from anyone who strayed away from the norm, whether it was in relation to mental health or not. This supports the theory driven argument that policy making consists of a set of hypotheses that relates a programme to a context - and the key to evaluation is therefore to test the hypotheses (Shaw, 1997).

Probing for Cause: Quasi/experimental evaluations utilising a mix of methodologies can often produce a number of competing explanations for any outcome identified. The problem is that there are often multiple causes for the success or otherwise of a programme, not one single intervention.

However, one such example is Taylor's (1975) well known scientific management evaluations. Particularly the famous pig-iron experiment with the great incentive worker Schmidt. Schmidt was one of a gang who hauled pig iron from factory to railroad car. What Taylor arranged was for his rate of pay to be increased providing he followed a pre-specified work plan rather than humping the stuff to his own pace. There followed a huge and demonstrable change in output. Even though this is not a strictly controlled experiment, the previous regularities are so well documented and the change so marked that the connection between incentives and output was held to be proven. However, such causal explanations are rarely this clear. More often than not a range of rival theories exist to account for the observed change (or non-change) and the requisite approach is to assess which of these rival theories are most plausible.

However, one of the advantages of knowing what the 'goals' or 'theory' of the programme are in advance is that the existence of rival explanations can assist stakeholders in examining their assumptions about the linkages and activities necessary for the achievement of the desired outcomes. This is what Suchman (1967) termed the programmes 'validity assumptions' or beliefs about the cause and effect relationships in place. Suchman took the example of epilepsy to illustrate the point. Epilepsy decision makers assume that publications in academic journals convey new knowledge to medical practitioners. However, does such a causal linkage hold true? For example many interventions or programmes for social change are built upon the assumption that; first, new information leads to attitude change; and two, attitude change leads to behavioural change. Although such assumptions are testable it is not possible to test all the validity assumptions within a programme or evaluate all of the causal linkages in a programme theory of action:

It is impossible to secure proof of the effectiveness of everything one wishes to do. Nor is it desirable. Operating personnel must proceed on the basis of the best desirable knowledge at the time.
(Suchman, 1967, p.43)

Patton suggests that evaluators should consequently work with the primary intended information users to identify these critical validity assumptions where reduction of uncertainty about causal linkages could make the most difference (Patton, 1986).

Intended and Unintended Outcome Analysis: This approach argues that programmes are not variables but processes and that outcomes should not be assessed in terms of whether the goal of the programme has been achieved but in terms of a multiplicity of outcomes - including unintended outcomes. Qualitative evaluation research lay claim to be able to identify unintended outcomes. Such a claim is also made by theory driven evaluation. Here stakeholder consultation requires them all to make recommendations on what outcomes to examine. However, the theory adopted by the evaluation will often, in itself, enable an identification of potential outcomes to monitor. Indeed, the idea of 'unintended consequences' is one of the cornerstones of Gidden's 'Structuration Theory' (1970). Here Gidden's examined dependency between human agency and social structure - structures produce action. The structural properties of the social system provides the means by which people act and are also the outcomes of those actions. In addition middle-range theory can often be developed from existing research reports which impinge on current work.

Intervening Mechanism Evaluation: The basic concept is that a causal connection between events is difficult to establish by examining data relating to those events. Further information regarding the underlying process or *mechanism* which connects events has often to be applied. In research it is difficult to understand the outcome of a policy without knowing how it relates to different interests and actions of various stakeholders. In public policy the key evaluation question is 'what changes should this policy bring about?'. In creating change which will affect the public the key is to induce a change in the thinking and the action of the recipients of the programme. This often entails a knowledge of people's goals, motivations, cultural resources, economic and social situations. The evaluation would then involve understanding how the policy brought about a change in these. Public policy may change people's thinking and the choices they make. However, individual choices are rarely simple but are brought about through multiple causal channels. A feature of human decision making is that it often ends up a process of choice - which often works in a kind of 'on the one hand and then again on the other' framework. Choice often involves counteractions.

A public policy or programme will often trigger competing or even contradictory impulses. This is well documented in economics. One anti-inflationary policy is to increase interest rates. This sets in motion opposite effects. One is that people borrow and spend less - demand is reduced and prices either fall or fail to rise at the same rate. The other is that interest rate rises are inflationary in themselves. The cost of living (especially mortgages) go up and people chase more income (which is inflationary) to catch up with inflation. The way people make decisions depends upon a variety of other circumstances. As a consequence, theory laden evaluation attempts to identify which of these decision making processes (underlying mechanisms) are actually set in motion in order to establish patterns of causation.

Unfortunately this goal is actually futile because it is a misreading of the goals of science. Even a universal law in natural science is not a law that is always true. A universal law is one which is always present *in the conditions specified*. Pawson & Tilley cite a good example:

> ...think of perhaps the best known of all the regularities in physics, that governing the relationship between the temperature, volume and pressure of a fixed mass of gas (PV/T=constant). We regard this as the 'gas law' even though we know that this equation of the constant conjunction between these variables holds for only a limited range of their values are nevertheless prepared to speak without hesitation of, say, an increase in pressure causing an increase in temperature and are persuaded that such a relationship comprises a 'law of nature' because we have established a comprehensive model of the mechanisms and contextual conditions which bind together these elements of a system.
> (Pawson & Tilley, 1997, p.58)

The basic point here is that natural laws are not universally applicable but apply in certain conditions and these conditions are produced by theory.

Pawson and Tilley go on to argue that evaluations need to understand the relationship between mechanism, regularity and context. The lesson for practice is that evaluations should specifying the contexts in which a public policy or programme will work. The argument is that evaluation should move towards a matching of the outcomes to the mechanism and the context. I would argue because of this, Evaluation is not about establishing generalisable findings, because there may well be none to be made. That is not to argue that there are no regularities. Patterns and themes do exist - the argument is that the key issue is to tightly specify the contexts in which public programmes will work. The implications for policy is that 'broad brush' policies will tend to be less successful because they are going to cross-cut contexts and mechanisms which will often change over time.

I would go further and argue that more focussed programmes could be more cost effective as they will enhance change in those groups which will benefit from the programme. For those unlikely to benefit it may be cost effective to focus a different programme tailored more to their situation. This is an argument which is quite often difficult to fight because political considerations often demand uniformity of treatment. Indeed political considerations can be very influential in evaluation as is illustrated in the case studies discussed in later chapters.

2 Issues in Evaluating Public Policy

Evaluation of public policy is somewhat less well established than evaluation of programs. Some of the key issues in policy evaluation will be outlined briefly here. This changes the focus of discussion to include the nature of policy making as well as issues in evaluation strategy and methodology. There seems to be a consensus, particularly amongst senior civil servants that we know what policy making is. However, there are a number of different theories on how and where policy is made and our choice can impact upon the evaluation strategy and this will be explored briefly.

There seem to be three broad policy evaluation approaches which are not, of course, discrete. The first approach examines the effectiveness of policy, whether the policy is working and if not the reasons for policy failure. A number of papers have looked at this. The second approach examines the distributional outcomes and effects of policy (or who gains and loses and by how much), and the third examines value for money. The main difference between the first two approaches is that distribution can be assessed without any knowledge of the aims of policy whereas effectiveness can only be assessed in relation to a set of policy goals. The problem is that public policies commonly lack detailed objectives against which they can be judged. If we believed the television show *Yes, Prime Minister* the reason for this would be obvious:

> Governments don't spend money to achieve anything; spending is symbolic; they spend money to show what they believe in.

There is some truth in these comments. The approach is seen, for instance, in arguments to devote a particular share of GDP to 'worthy' causes such as 'overseas aid' or 'expenditure on scientific projects'. However, evaluating effectiveness is greatly facilitated, to say the least, if there are a clear set of goals. There is also some evidence that Governments, faced with budget constraints and too many spending desires, are becoming increasingly interested in what effects they are achieving with public spending. Systematic assessment of effectiveness should involve the following features:

1.   identifying and examining the target group at which the policy is aimed;
2.   the consequences both for that group and for other groups; and
3.   the extent to which the consequences matched the policy objectives.

The difficulties discussed in the previous chapter, in terms of fairly discrete programme interventions become more than just magnified when we examine broader brush 'people' policies which cross cut contexts, social and political groupings and cultures. In this case all three of these elements present problems for policy evaluation. First, the group most effected is not always easy to identify and this is particularly the case when the evaluation would require private information about individual citizens or even nation states. Second, the consequences of policy are sometimes hard to identify, particularly when the policy has a general impact upon the whole society or wider world. This is because of numerous intervening variables which are themselves difficult to identify and weight. Third, measuring the consequences against the original policy objectives, as we have discussed, is difficult when the policies themselves can lack specific, measurable goals.

One consequence of these difficulties is that a great deal of policy evaluation has been crude and unsystematic. One approach I have sometimes adopted has been to evaluate against the underlying theory or the assumptions upon which the policy is based. Recent initiatives such as the Comprehensive Spending Review, and the establishment of indicators for examining Resource Accounting and Budgeting will provide a basis against which costs could be allocated and performance measured. However, historically, policy evaluation has often taken a 'back seat' in the search for economies and this is in part due to the lack of clear policy objectives.

For example (and this will be discussed in more depth in a later chapter), Political disillusionment in the ability of the UK welfare state to impact significantly upon disadvantage and poverty within society has gradually led to a shift in focus of services away from achieving positive change and towards the maintenance of social problems at manageable levels. The issue which this shift has raised is the level at which disadvantage and other social problems should be maintained. This change of emphasis, well documented in the evaluation literature (cf. Weiss, 1990), has in practical terms indicated a move away from effectiveness and the achievement of organisational goals towards the use of economy and efficiency as main evaluation criteria.

There are also, of course, a number of other difficulties in evaluating policy.

1. Most evaluations start from the assumption that benefits and costs are recognisable entities. In practice, however, it may be very difficult to draw the line between costs and benefits. For example, some costs can also be benefits. Some radical examples to illustrate the point: Ivan Ilich challenges the whole nature of organised medical care as a benefit, claiming that medics are actually a cause of ill-health and that better health has resulted not from their activities but from improved diets, housing conditions, public health action etc. Of course, Ilich, ignores important medical and pharmacological developments but he does so to make a point - and it is a point which is not without merit. An equally radical attack on the alleged benefits of education can also be mounted by arguing that its prime purpose is not to educate but to indoctrinate, socialise and repress individual initiative. In this fashion a commonly recognised benefit becomes a cost - depending upon ones standpoint. Benefits in this view are value judgements. The problem becomes even more complex when it comes to identifying and assessing intangible benefits and costs - such as achieving status in the world, or personal security - which may be no less important than tangible ones. There is also an understandable tendency to see the minister as the key stakeholder in policy evaluation. However, consultation with other stakeholders can be important in clarifying policy benefits.

2. A second problem follows on from the first. If it is assumed that it is possible to define and locate costs and benefits, evaluators are then faced with the problem of valuing them. Ideally a numerical measurement of some description is needed. Even with tangible costs and benefits we have seen from a number of papers that this can be difficult. Intangible and symbolic policies such as creating an enterprise culture, or ensuring that Britain is hitting above its weight in the World are even harder to value.

Problems in establishing the distributional effects of policy are also important - but these arise from technical issues on measurement, and are less fundamental:

3. The 'accounting units' chosen are important. For example, how can the UK's 53 million citizens be accurately classified? This is traditionally done by social class or occupation or by geographical location - or by demographic characteristics such as age, sex or household size. The choice made will affect the findings of the research. For example, if a comparison of North and South in the UK is required where does the North start? (York? Nottingham? Or the Watford Gap?)

4. There are also difficulties in deciding a timescale for measurement - what would we mean by 'medium' or 'long term' for example. The choice could be important as distributional patterns and outcomes can change over time.

These issues are fundamental, but in practice not insoluble. However, it should be recognised that their resolution often involves value judgements at some level - which should be grounded in experience.

The 'value for money' approach is perhaps most reflected in the work of the National Audit office. *The National Audit Office* (NAO). The nature of the NAO's work was defined in the National Audit Act in 1983, which stated:

> The Comptroller and Auditor General may carry out examinations into the economy, efficiency and effectiveness with which any department... has used its resources in discharging its functions.

These are termed Value for Money (VFM) studies. However, the NAO may not question the merits of policy decisions, which means that the NAO's role is restricted to examining policy implementation.

The VFM studies have two main objectives:
1.   To provide Government with independent information, advice and assurance, and;
2.   To help audited bodies improve their performance in achieving VFM.

The NAO reports on activities which, in their opinion, lead to sub-optimal use of public resources and their studies are focussed around the achievement of the '3 E's' (Economy, Efficiency and Effectiveness). Their reports have to be readily understood by parliament and are consequently not usually highly technical. Example of some VFM questions in the health service are listed below:

Economy: was equipment bought at minimum cost?, are buildings and maintenance costs minimised?
Efficiency: could the appointments system be changed so that more patients could be seen by the same number of doctors?
Effectiveness: what is the quality of the service and how accessible is it?

The NAO's role is likely to develop in response to the major changes which have occurred in the organisation and funding of public services. These changes may include:

a) The increasing role of the private sector. At the moment the NAO has no statutory right of access to private firms involved in public services;
b) The recognition of the extent to which policies in one area of Government

activity affect those in others, for example in the arguments that the quality of education we give our children affects their employment prospects. The NAO's work may expand to allow it to comment on activities which cross cut departmental boundaries;

c) The introduction of output and performance assessment is recognised to reflect a general trend to manage by results rather than by compliance with process-based rules.

These changes will reflect a strengthening of accountability to Parliament. The White Paper on the NHS published in 1997 is a good example where the 'internal market' introduced by the last government is to be replaced in 1999 with what one might call a performance management framework. The Government has extended formal accountability for the use of resources right into primary care - to GPs - for the first time. Another example is the Dearing Report on Higher Education, which envisages strengthening accountability of universities to Parliament, partly through university management boards being formally accountable for their use of resources to the Public Accounts Committee. It is expected that the NAO will be diversifying its role within this new environment. However, (as will be discussed in more depth in the next chapter) a number of commentators have attempted to criticise the limitations of such a VFM approach and emphasise factors against which services should be evaluated - Equity and Humanity are such examples. This includes substantive and procedural justice where people may accept a negative outcome from a process perceived as fair.

In practice it is recognised that there is likely to be a trade-off between these various 'E's' and other values that enter into the decision about which elements of policy evaluation are to be given priority in any particular situation. What balance should there be between efficacy and economy, or being humane and being economic or effective? The action required to meet these various elements may coincide or may be in conflict - and if in conflict which is given priority? The answer to such questions is likely to rest on value judgements, which themselves are likely to vary according to situation and context.

In compiling such an assessment, it is usual to take into account three different aspects of the organisation: structure, process and outcome. However, it is often the case that an evaluation primarily concerned with concern for value for money may be ill suited to any assessment of, say, the humanity a service and may lack any real power to explain the relationships they find.

In my view, policy evaluation is about gaining understanding and learning. We need to understand the factors which influence a policy's success or failure in order to develop that and future policies. A value for money approach is important but this needs to be complementary to other approaches which have their primary focus on understanding process and structure. This brings me to just one of many alternative views of policy making.

Work by Etzioni recognises that the targets an organisation sets itself, may not be in line with externally imposed policy but are the results of a process of negotiation and conflict between groups within and outside of the organisation and are the outcome of process rather than formal function. This is also implied in the work of Michael Lipsky who goes so far as to argue that:

> ...the residual discretion enjoyed by workers who interact with and make decisions about clients results in workers effectively *making policy*... Their separate (aggregated) discretionary and unsanctioned behaviour adds to a patterned agency behaviour overall.
> (Lipsky, 1980, p.17)

This is not to say that executives can not influence policy:

> Executives can affect policy even though they can not intrude into the discretionary decision itself. They do this by attempting to increase the probability that outcomes, on the whole, will be more favourable to the preferred policy objective. They do this by shaping the environment in which (such) workers operate.
> (Lipsky, 1989, p.5)

This is particularly relevant in services which have a high level of devolved discretion and has a number of implications for policy analysis. First, will be some slippage between the policy preferred by the executive and the policy as implemented. Second, one has to examine the process by which the preferred policy is implemented to understand the influences on such workers/officials and how best to counter them. This brings us to a previously mentioned key issue in evaluation which is worth repeating here. The logic behind many outcome measures, league tables, and some other performance indicators are that the same intervention should always produce the same output. If it does not then the fault must lie in the quality of the service or policy. This is a problematic view of experimental logic and brings us to the question of the role and purpose of policy evaluation. Hogwood and Gunn (1984) argue that policy evaluation is important even though we live in a world of uncertainty where there is an imperfect or contested understanding of many issues, A key underlying question in their conception of evaluation is whether the particular policies under review have been successful in achieving the outcomes desired. This, of course, assumes that a set of desired outcomes has been drawn up by policy makers. Indeed they argue that policy and programmes should be designed in such a way as to be open to assessment by one evaluation technique or other. However, this is to suggest that the policy or programme design should be subservient to the methodology of evaluation.

A Policy Evaluation Case Study

McEldowney (1997) discusses the concepts of 'deadweight' and 'additionality' in the context of evaluation of an industrial development programme in Northern Ireland and is worth briefly reviewing here. This was a £94 million, 5-year industrial development operational programme, which commenced in 1990, and was a form of community assistance from the EC structural funds. The programme aimed to:

a) improve the competitiveness of indigenous industry
b) encourage additional small enterprises
c) the attraction of mobile projects into Northern Ireland
d) assist the development of management and workforce skills
e) provide an infrastructure to support industrial **development.**

The Northern Ireland Economic Research Centre (NIERC) was appointed as external evaluator. There were several immediate evaluation problems: a multiplicity of services; a wide spectrum of industrial development policies were generated over the 5-year period; The evaluation commenced 18 months after the start of the programme; a value for money audit was to be included. The evaluation sought to address a number of issues including:

• the extent to which the programmes structure and strategy were appropriate to the needs of the region
• micro and macro economic impact
• lessons for future regional development
• was the programme appropriate to the policy
• the extent to which the programme succeeded in levering up further investment (additionality)
• the extent to which expenditure was directed to recipients other than those directed (deadweight).

The evaluation found a high level of deadweight associated with the assistance. The study found that 49 percent of companies would not have reduced expenditure levels in the absence of such assistance, whilst 56 percent of companies reported that such assistance either had 'no influence' or only 'some influence' on the final decision to invest (Sheehan, 1993). Moreover, without the assistance 57 percent of companies would not have reduced the quality of their investment. A further study by the Northern Ireland Audit Office estimated a level of deadweight of 62 percent whilst the job creation figures only reached 25 percent of target figures (1993). These findings raise serious doubts on the value for money of such policies. Further doubts arose in a study by Roper (1993) which suggested that the direct financial assistance to firms had the effect of raising profit levels. Such findings could have a very negative effect and could lead to serious policy conclusions about the benefit of such, highly expensive, policies. McEldowney's work attacks the methodological limitations of deadweight and additionality in evaluation and the emphasis given to it in the evaluation reports. He also argues for proper operationalisation of such concepts in a way that recognises the importance of decision making and why certain decisions are taken. He argues that most evaluations of grant assistance fail to recognise this and instead tend to focus upon a crude counterfactual question which does little to illuminate the range of influences and processes explaining either an investment decision or the role of grant assistance.

In other words, in focussing on outputs and ignoring the contexts in which the policy has been enacted the policy programme is treated as a separate variable, separated from its context, for the purposes of analysis. Evaluation should be about learning and understanding how policy works, or does not work, and thus feed into policy development and learning. This would focus more upon the purpose of evaluation, not as an end in itself, but as a means of gaining information for decision making.

3 Defining the Goals of Public Services

Political disillusionment in the ability of the UK welfare state to impact significantly upon disadvantage and poverty within society has gradually led to a shift in focus of services away from achieving positive change and towards the maintenance of social problems at manageable levels. Over the last couple of decades it has become common currency, across the political spectrum to suggest that the welfare state is in a 'crisis'. A number of prognoses have abounded which have predicted the imminent demise of the structures set up and developed since 1948, or even of liberal democracy itself, crushed under the burden of misplaced, monolithic altruism and welfare dependency. However, whilst commentators on social policy have been in broad agreement, particularly since the mid 1970s, that 'something is rotten in the state of welfare', there has been precious little consensus on what that 'something' actually is. A part of the problem stems from terminology. As Pierson (1998) has pointed out, although most writers on the welfare state use a common terminology in their critiques of it, this terminology is not consistently used. The very word 'crisis', used to sum up the essential underlying 'rottenness' of the modern welfare system, seems conceptually to mean different things to different commentators. Just as intellectually pernicious is the idea of 'contradiction' used in structural critiques of welfare provision by Marxists and neo-liberals alike that, once again, has ambiguous usage. One common theme, in writing on the welfare state is the postulated post-war 'golden age' of welfare (beginning at the systems inception and ending variously at any time from the early 1960s to the late 1970s) has come to an end. It thus follows that a new approach to welfare provision is needed in the modern world, in which many of the assumptions of 'welfarism' - e.g. the absolute predominance of patriarchal family units, or the possibility of full employment as a goal for economic policy - no longer hold true. Conclusion on how this new approach might be structured draw upon very disparate intellectual sources.

Pierson (1998) and others have extensively rehearsed the details of particular crisis theories. However a concern of this paper is the context in which crisis theories arise, rather than the theories themselves. A crisis mentality in academic circles has created a vibrant 'problem-solving' discourse, and different views of crisis make for different interpretations of its solution. Some commentators, such as Friedman (1962) and Hayek (1976), see it as a moral crisis with fiscal consequences; more recent writers have framed it in the context of theories of modernity. Both suggest practical solutions, and policy practitioners are left with the task of assessing their relative merits.

'Crisis' can be a misleading word in the context of much of the social policy literature on the welfare state. Pierson, for example, suggests a four part typology:

> A long-standing, perhaps concealed, struggle or set of 'contradictions' which emerge and must be definitively resolved in the present, as for example the 'class struggle' thesis of Gough (1979); An internal catastrophe brought about by exogenous phenomena, such as the effect on the economy of the rapid increase in oil costs in the mid 1970s; A deep-seated contradiction, existing within an institutional structure, which becomes a destructive force and causes the demise of that structure, corresponding to the neo-liberal view of the dichotomy of the market and statutory redistribution; Or, in common parlance, it can simply refer to any large scale problem.
> (Pierson,1998, p.138)

This highlights that there may be a variance of views on what form a crisis may take. Equally, many of the crises postulated by theorists have not come to pass. Although some of the forecasts for the future of the welfare state made in the 1970s were positively apocalyptic, these have not survived the test of history. Despite economic shocks and the end of rapid economic growth in the last two decades, neither the welfare state nor liberal democracy has collapsed around our ears. Nevertheless, although welfare democracies have proven themselves to be of reasonably sound structure, the critique from both left and right has not lost momentum. The agreement on a 'crisis theory of the Welfare State' has remained a powerful one as welfare costs seem to fall short of requirements and the so-called 'dependency culture' becomes entrenched. Whilst it could be argued that reports of the 'slow death of welfare' have been exaggerated, the welfare state still faces quite considerable problems. For example, at the time of writing The Secretary of State for Health, Frank Dobson, admitted that the NHS was in crisis. Newspapers have shown people queuing for hours on hospital trolleys and much has been made of the need for more resources, for nurses, beds, doctors and equipment.

Politicians are often inclined to see the problems of the welfare system as primarily fiscal, i.e. related to questions of afford ability. This was, of course, a major consideration in the attempts of the Conservative administrations of the 1980's to 'roll back the boundaries of the state'. However, despite their efforts to control spending, many commentators have noted that spending on social security actually increased during the 1980s, linked to high levels of unemployment. Indeed many welfare structures proved highly resilient to change for a number of reasons. These include the political risks of public opposition to 'retrenchment', the prohibitive costs of fully privatised alternatives, and what Glennerster (1997) calls the 'inertia' of social provision already on the statute books (social programmes already legislated for are hard to adapt or remove without political cost, and may have long time scales built into their administrative mechanisms).

Pierson argues that the Conservative administrations of the 1980s, if public opinion had allowed, would have pursued policy goals in tune with their ideology. The central view then held was that the welfare state was one of the primary causes of economic stagnation, in that it was expensive to run and stifled individual responsibility and enterprise. Conservatives, whether traditional or neo-liberal, are not in principle opposed to inequality, and thus their ideal welfare state would have been an entirely means tested one containing as few legislative instruments of redistribution as possible (Pierson, 1994, p.6), as opposed to one which emphasised universalist benefit payments. Indeed, universal programmes of income support, for example child benefit, were attacked most vigorously in the attempt to reduce social spending as their demise evinces the least public outcry and can be justified on the basis of 'targeting need'. Equally, incremental changes in entitlements and payment values were used to further reduce benefit spending whilst avoiding extensive disquiet. However, the success of those Conservative administrations in bringing down spending levels is open to debate. For example, legislation enacted in 1986 made possible an annual reduction of £700 million in social security funding. This seemingly large sum represented less than 2 percent of the total social security spend in 1987-8 and has been argued to be more for political concerns rather than a serious attempt to address 'fiscal crisis' (Pierson, 1994).

This would suggest that a primarily fiscal approach is a limited solution and that new discourses need developing. Indeed, the very existence of a fiscal crisis has been questioned. Critics of welfare tend to claim that the rising costs of provision have endangered its prospects for sustainability in the long-term and that it will eventually bankrupt the state. Hills, however, has shown that welfare expenditure remained largely stable as a percentage of GDP throughout the 1970s and 1980s. Whilst a 4 percent growth between 1992-93 seemed alarming at the time, Hills argued that continued growth at that level was unlikely (Hills, 1993). One lesson which can perhaps be gained from the 1980s is that the 'inertia' of social programmes precludes any dramatic spending reductions in the short term and may also prevent dramatic increases in the welfare bill.

Although total welfare spending remained largely static, a change in the structure of that spending is clearly visible. The main growth areas within the total budget were health and social security. Whilst few would argue the necessity of health are spending, the growth in social security has been a target of critics. Hayek, one of the most influential figures in neo-liberal thought, argues in 'The mirage of social justice' that a State which enacts legislation with universally redistributive goals is inclined towards totalitarianism in its rejection of free human action, and is therefore of itself undesirable (Hayek, 1976). Even commentators sympathetic to welfare provision have been alarmed by the trend within welfare spending towards 'safety-net' benefits such as income support and have begun to accept parts of Hayek's critique. Rather than seeing a fiscal crisis in the welfare state they prefer to look upon the problem as a dichotomy between its original aims and the structure of post-modern society.

Giddens (1994) discusses in detail some of the assumptions upon which the welfare state was founded. One of these assumptions was mass employment, where 'employment' implied solely paid work within the labour market. Another was that of the nation state 'based on the economic centrality of mass production and the centralised organisation of capital and wage labour' (p.140). These two assumptions, it can be argued, have ceased to be valid. In particular 'globalisation', whilst one may be sceptical of its precise nature and influence, has had an effect upon the nation state's ability to regulate its own economic life. As new realities conflict with old certainties, so the argument runs, our perception of the welfare state must necessarily be open to reinterpretation. An important element in this discourse is contemporary ecological thought, which provides the theoretical underpinning of this 'uncertainty'. Readings of modernity and the risk inducing nature of 'humanism' like that of Ehrenfeld (1981) have been adapted into an overarching social theory by sociologists like Ulrich Beck. Modern society, for Beck, creates through the actions of its members, a new concept of risk, which he defines as 'a systematic way of dealing with hazards and insecurities induced and introduced by modernisation itself' (1992, p.21). This 'reflexive' risk rebounding on the very process that generates it, is one of the bases of Giddens welfare theory. Perhaps in a situation where the assumptions at the root of welfare systems have ceased to apply, welfare states instigate poverty at the same time as attempting to alleviate it. The largely predictable and generally short time span of unemployment, which should be a norm in an economy geared to mass employment, becomes unpredictable in a world where full employment can not be guaranteed, for reasons which arise from modernity itself - changes in production, the expansion of markets and so on. It is perhaps not so much rising costs and inability to meet them which is at issue so much as resources being organised in ways which are more and more inappropriate to the problems they were set up to meet (Giddens, 1994). Since welfare tends to be a system that compensates for the effects of 'external' hazards rather than militating

48

against their causes, it can not cope with *the manufactured* risk prevalent in postmodern society. This is best dealt with through 'positive', 'generative' and precautionary welfare measures and an improvement in what Giddens calls 'life politics' (1994, p.154). This is to say that problems traditionally dealt with through systems of state support can, perhaps, be better resolved by acting to influence lifestyles and life choice, rather than merely doling out money a posteriori when things go wrong. Influencing the life choices of individuals is seen as a desirable step towards individual management of risk.

The move towards a consensus on issues of welfare pluralism such as these, which Powell and Hewitt have observed (1998) may be an effect of what they call 'liberal capitalist hegemony'. Crouch has more trenchantly described it as a neo-liberal consensus in which barriers between left and right are broken down many of the tenants of free market thinkers are accepted as primary assumptions. Fiscal prudence, minimal government intervention, low taxation and depressed public spending are all watchwords of this approach (Crouch, 1997). Equally, social policy is seen as subordinate to market goals. In the subtext of much current writing on the future of welfare, the tax and spend universal welfare state providing subsistence support is replaced by pragmatic welfare systems, which are determined by the primacy of market value against ideological commitments like redistribution. The 'risk management' model of welfare provision is fundamentally not redistributive, in the sense that redistribution is seen as overly deterministic. Giarini and Stahel (1989) argue the idea that modern societal and economic development depends not so much on achieving perfect, deterministic and sure objectives but rather on developing creative activities in a world where uncertainty and risk are a given condition. The implication is that individual creativity in the provision of personal welfare is the ideal form of social insurance. The risk management model, however, is not immune to problems of its own.

The most obvious form of risk management that an individual can adopt is personal insurance. Many people in the UK have, indeed, already been encouraged to supplement state pension provision with private policy, for example as the likely costs of an ageing population become apparent. It is clear, however, that a purely private system of provision can not offer the same level of value for money as is offered by the state at present. For example large-scale privatisation of health care has not taken place because of the prohibitive costs of such a measure - it costs the United States over twice as much public expenditure to support a private system (with tax expenditures and covering the provision of those uninsured). Similarly, if individuals were required to obtain private cover for the eventualities of unemployment, ill health, and long term care, the total cost to a person on average earnings (£400 per week) in a low risk insurance category would be just over £1,000 per year. This is, in itself, not an inconsiderable sum, and if we consider that the cost to a similar individual of a 1p change in the basic rate of income tax would be £150 per year, the advantages of a nationally administered scheme levied through increased base rates of taxation, as against personal provision, become obvious (Hills and Burchardt, 1997). It could be

49

argued that if there is a 'fiscal crisis' in the welfare state then advocacy of private welfare provision is simply a move to shift that crisis from a collective to an individual context, which would make a nonsense of shared risk arguments.

However, it is not simply the mechanics of such a measure which are problematic. Many of the arguments by Giddens and others are based on influencing life choices of individuals in an attempt to empower them to face the risks posited by modernity. These arguments beg the question: how should public authorities legislate for lifestyle, which often borders upon areas of personal morality? The present labour government, elected on a 'middle way' platform which drew on many of Giddens ideas of citizenship and social responsibility, has attempted to exert influence on the areas of 'life politics' he discusses - government proposals for the welfare-to-work scheme and parenting classes to reduce the rate of family break up are some of the more obvious examples. One of the examples which Giddens gives of an area in which lifestyle choices could be influenced by policy is tobacco advertising. Giddens advocates a ban on all such advertising on the grounds that it would be comparatively inexpensive to the exchequer, and would have a positive influence on the number of people admitted to the NHS for smoking related cancers. Prevention in Giddens model of generative welfare is always better than cure. While this seems a simple and effective experience has shown that where powerful interest groups are involved existing non-risk-averse modes of life politics have their defenders. The Labour government's recent U-turn on proposals to curb tobacco sponsorship of Formula One racing clearly illustrated the problems of implementing these kinds of generative measures in the context of polity where power relations and the need to attract funding remain important.

Another example of the problems inherent in the application of risk management tactics to social policy is shown by the proximity of Giddens life politics to recent writings on the dependency culture. He sees work as a form of self-definition, following Beck's concept of risk management as dependent on the individual as centre of action and the shaping of self 'biography' (Beck, 1992). Giddens postulates that the dependency culture arises from the conflict between the full employment assumption and the social isolation caused by unmanaged risk (1994) and that a generative approach would be one which attempted to institute a 'politics of second chances' - perhaps analogous with the rhetoric of 'a hand up, not a hand out' for those caught in the trap which such a dichotomy entails. One obvious policy application of this would seem to be 'welfare to work', a central part of the present government's 'new deal' where benefit receipt is made conditional upon proof that the recipient is actively seeking work. Laurence Mead, in a study for the IEA, argues that changes in social arrangements and income distribution (the aims of welfare universalism) can not eradicate poverty. He argues the only response is to put in place statutory instruments to counteract what he calls 'self defeating actions by poor people themselves, particularly single parents, non-work and crime' (1994, p.13) through incentives and sanctions. However, the very concept of the dependency culture which Giddens seems to accept as a given, has been questioned. It has been pointed out that the 'underclass', the posited victim group of the dependency trap, is defined teleologically by most writers who have studied its existence. The frequently cited variables which characterise this class are both the cause and the effect of its existence, in that exclusion from the labour market is generally seen, for example, both as a cause of crime and caused by crime (Dean and Taylor-Gooby, 1992). While generative values can be of some use in tackling the problems of the poor, it should be noted that such schemes as welfare to work, which accept the underclass thesis, are often punitive and based upon Charles Murray's assertion that we should be less ready to benefit recipients 'victims' - an assertion which many practitioners may find unacceptable.

The theory of uncertainty posited by Beck, which Giddens attempts to transform into a practical policy strategy, faces a further problem. He presumes that the citizen can be made to adjust to risk and can be directed towards life choices which empower them to face risk head on. However, the example he gives of avoidance of cancer risk through smoking, passive or active, is an example of risk averse behaviour where risk is known. The very nature of the kind of uncertainty he describes is that it can not be quantified. For Beck, who provides his model of risk, every human action has the potential to be risky. His postulate for a welfare system based upon the recognition of risk all carry the subtext that risk, in some sense, can still be known. However, we can not predict the future and thus people can not design their own risk-aware 'life politics' to a sufficient degree. A system which compensate for the results of risk, such as the one we have at present, must remain primary. There is equally the issue of information deficit. If people are not made aware of strategies for confronting risk, the cost to the individual of the consequences could be considerable. Risk discrepancy is also likely to run on class lines, which can be seen from the model of relative gains and losses under a private insurance system for various income groups. As Hills and Burchardt (1997) point out, risk is not evenly distributed throughout the population. As a consequence, the move towards risk management is an important step away from obsession with fiscal matters, but this discourse can only be a guide to, not a blueprint for, policy development into the next millennium.

One issue these shifts have raised is the way in which welfare programmes should be evaluated. This change of emphasis, well documented in the evaluation literature (cf. Weiss, 1990), has in practical terms indicated a move away from effectiveness and the achievement of organisational goals towards the use of economy and efficiency as main evaluation criteria. This was accompanied in UK health and social care services by market reforms. Evaluation has not yet reinvented itself to full evaluate policy and programmes arising from current theories, though there are indications of change.

At the centre of the market reforms in welfare lies the distinct split between purchaser and provider functions which was aimed at developing competition in the supply of services. It was hoped that this would result in greater efficiencies and better quality as services became more responsive to client needs. Although

51

the market may indeed be more efficient, there are difficulties in terms of quality assurance and evaluation. In particular, there is a concern over the relative access to information. The separation of these functions has led to a situation where the main source of information for the evaluation of providers' activity (including service quality) is actually from data supplied by the providers themselves. The concern exists that providers may be able to engage in low quality services and for the purchaser to be unaware of this situation unless some crisis exists. This has led to the development of government outcome measures and performance indicators to evaluate services.

This chapter argues the form that service evaluation takes can have a major impact upon service development. In particular, it is argued that current systems of evaluation have the potential of mistaking efficiency for quality. The consequences of this for evaluation practice is discussed.

The Rise of the 'E's'

The UK government's concern over expenditure of the public sector generally, and the health and social services in particular, became focussed around what has become known as the '3 E's' - Economy, Efficiency and Effectiveness (Metcalfe & Richards, 1990). A major criticism of health and social care services was that they were judged to be inefficient in terms of providing an optimal level of services for a given amount of resources. For the government the clearest indication of this inefficiency was the way in which resources were allocated each year, not according to assessed need, but by simply adding an inflationary increment to the previous years budget (Glennerster, 1997). From the early 1980s government has been concerned that public services should be managed in order to meet these '3 E's'. However, a number of commentators have attempted to emphasise other factors as the basis for evaluating human services. For example Cochrane (1971) cites Effectiveness, Efficiency and Equity as the three dimensions on which any human service organisation should be evaluated. In Cochrane's view a service is equitable if it is equally available to all those who need it. Strong and Dingwall (1989) add Humanity to Cochrane's three dimensions. In their view a service is humane if both clients and staff are treated in a civilised fashion. In practice it is recognised that there is likely to be a trade-off between these various dimensions and other values that enter into the decision about which are to be given priority in any particular situation (Dingwall, 1992).

In compiling this assessment, it is usual to take into account three different aspects of the organisation: structure, process and outcome (Donabedian, 1976). However, recent experience in the UK has been dominated by outcome evaluation. The concern has particularly focussed upon what outcomes are possible from a given set of resources (efficiency). This reflects the ascendency of utilitarian approaches to social analysis, especially from neo-classical economics, which does not acknowledge any influences intervening between individuals and the incentives and sanctions of the market or its proxy in the shape of the performance indicators imposed upon them. Such an approach highlights the importance of efficiency but is ill suited to any assessment of the humanity of a service and lacks any real power to explain the relationships they find (Dingwall, 1992). The link between resources and outcomes is left vague. The argument of this paper is that the overall mission or goals of health and social care services are being subsumed to drives for efficiency and that the way services are evaluated is assisting this trend. Evaluation, as we have seen, has been defined as:

> An attempt to measure the extent to which outcomes can be validly correlated with inputs and/or outputs.
> (Rutman, 1984, p.12)

This emphasises that the focus of evaluation is about causation. In the view expressed by Rutman evaluation is interested in cause and effect relationships. After all, health and social services are meant to promote some change in society and the degree to which that change is affected is important. However, as pointed out earlier, the other part of evaluation is what is it for:

> The purpose of evaluation research is to measure the effects of a programme against the goals it set out to accomplish as a means of contributing to subsequent decision making about the programme and improving future programming.
> (Weiss, 1990, p.21)

Evaluation and Organisations Theory

Evaluation of welfare services in the United Kingdom is generally more in line with Rutman's view of evaluation in that it matches outcomes with resources and compares outcomes between services and programmes within a context of fixed budgets. However, for welfare it could be argued that Weiss's view should have more importance as it emphasises the need to include progress towards the change in society which the services were put in place to achieve. The argument of this paper is that current forms of evaluation which are based primarily on outcome are problematic because they do not fully incorporate realisation of organisational goals (effectiveness).

The concept of goals occupies an ambiguous position in organisational analysis in that it is both a central analytical point and an ill-defined concept. Thompson suggests that the modern organisation has always been:

> ...an instrument, a deliberate and rational means for attaining known goals. In some versions the goals are explicitly stated:

53

in others the goals are assumed to be self-evident as, for example the goal of the private business firm is to maximise profits.
(Thompson, 1967, p.397)

Although it is generally accepted in the literature that every organisation has a goal, or set of goals, this has often become a taken for granted assumption (Morgan, 1990). Empirical investigation has shown that what Georgiou (1973) referred to as 'the classic goal paradigm' has flaws. In particular many of the key goals of a welfare organisation will be set outside of the organisation itself, for example by government ministers. The acceptability of those goals to the members of the organisation may place limits upon how they are adopted and pursued. For example, externally imposed goals are often too ambitious or vague to be measured. Rosenbaum, commenting upon crime prevention programmes makes a parallel point that public services often try to fit citizens into services rather than fitting services to suit the needs of citizens. The implication is that welfare services may be too unresponsive:

> We are past the point of wanting to report that crime prevention does or does not work, and now are interested in specifying the conditions under which particular outcomes are observed.
> (Rosenbaum, 1988, p.382)

This is perhaps a particular issue with regard to the achievement of welfare goals and leads to problems in the judging of organisational success. Another issue is that producers may interpret or operationalise goals in ways which best suits them rather than the people whose needs the service was intended to meet.

Etzioni has used the metaphor of the electric light which functions at low efficiency to illustrate this point. A great deal of the energy going into a light bulb produces heat rather than light making the light bulb relatively ineffective in terms of its goals. There is little public concern on this. Light bulbs are judged in comparison to other types of light bulb to discover the most effective and efficient. This illustrates that such concepts as economy and efficiency are commonly determined by relative rather than absolute standards. In much of the British welfare system services are judged by league tables which illustrate relative positions against some narrow set of performance criteria. With Schools it is exam results, with Universities it is research income and publications and with health and social services it is performance against indicators such as Citizens Charter targets. Etzioni goes on to argue that goals may not always be at the forefront of an organisation's efforts:

> An organisational goal is a desired state of affairs which an organisation attempts to realise. The organisational goal is that

54

future state of affairs which the organisation as a collectivity
is trying to bring about.
(Etzioni, 1964, p.6)

In other words the official objective is overcome and in its place is a conception of goals that arise through empirical investigation or impinging reality. In health and social care the impinging reality is the extremely tight budgetary constraints which dominate service planning against a background of high demand. Etzioni recognises that the targets an organisation sets itself are not the real goals but are the result of a process of negotiation and conflict between groups within and outside of the organisation and the outcome of process rather than formal function (Vecchio, 1991). However, there is a danger that the original or real goal will become lost to the organisation. This issue has not been successfully addressed in the organisations literature. What is more, new approaches in organisations theory have shown the negotiated basis of any organisational goals. There has traditionally been a sharp line drawn between the study of social and formal organisations (Benson, 1977). Formal organisations were seen as rational and goal oriented and stressed a system of rules for the pursuit of those goals (Hassard, 1990). However, this began to be questioned in the 1970s:

The realm of rules could thus be usefully pictured as a tiny
island of structured stability around which swirled and beat a
vast ocean of negotiation. But we would push the metaphor
further and assert what is already implicit in our own
discussion: that there is *only* vast ocean.
(Strauss, 1978, p.313)

This is the starting point of much of contemporary organisation theory, which acknowledges the importance of extra situational influences (Dingwall & Strong, 1985; Hassard & Pym, 1990). It is also recognised that formal organisations must sustain an image of rational conduct to maintain their social legitimacy and that members produce arguments that will be externally sanctionable and actions that are logically congruent with the means/ends scheme thus depicted. This organisational theory does not go as far as Strauss, as it retains the distinction between formal and social organisation, but restates it as a difference in verbal accounting practices rather than in substance. However, the advocates of this approach have failed to address crucial methodological questions on how organisations can best be studied and evaluated - though Dingwall and Strong (1985) argue against outcome based measures and in favour of ethnographic approaches.

These problems of defining organisations and the parameters by which they should be evaluated have not been acknowledged by government. With strict cash limits imposed on services this would seem to reinforce the difference between what services can achieve and policy goals. As a result the role of the services are increasingly open to interpretation by producers. The government has attempted to compare the performance of services against each other but little attempt has been made to evaluate the success of a service against organisational goals (however defined). An examination of the way in which service quality is evaluated perhaps best highlights the main issues.

Quality

Service quality has always been an issue in health and social care services, though the current popularity of the term seems to have come from concerns in the private market about the quality of goods. In the private market quality is perceived by the consumer. In this respect quality is a broad concept. A washing machine may work well and be reliable but unless it is attractively designed and backed up by good after sales service it is not regarded as a quality product. The setting of quality standards in the private sector is meant to be achieved by continuous reference to the consumer about their wants and needs for a service. However are such concepts wholly appropriate to public services generally and health and social care services in particular?

Amongst the difficulties of adopting such an approach is concern over the ways in which consumer satisfaction can be manipulated. For example if expectations of a service are high and the perceived quality is moderate then satisfaction will be low. On the other hand if expectations are low then even a poor service can result in consumer satisfaction. One could argue that perceived service cut backs over a number of years have lead the public to lower their expectations of the quality of services. There is also an issue over how quality links into service demand. In the private sector a quality service will increase demand for that service which will, in turn, increase the profits for the company providing that service. In the public sector, on the other hand, if high quality led to increased demand this would draw upon public finances and what would likely result is a lowering of quality as demand outstripped resources and rationing of service may even have to occur. In the health and social care services quality must be discussed within a context of resource limitations. This has led to arguments, particularly in the field of mental health, that while consumer satisfaction may be important the core focus of evaluation should be on outcomes not consumer perceptions of them (Shaw, 1997).

Quality: Differences Between Public and Private Sectors

This highlights the major difference between the public and private sectors, which is that public services aim to promote or maintain some change in society. For the NHS, for example, this outcome is in terms of improved health of the nation. This can lead to differing views on quality. The first is the provider view of quality which is related to outcome and where conformity to predetermined goals is the dominant aim. The user view of quality, on the other hand, will be informed by the process of service delivery and how the individual perceives that the service has responded to his/her needs. An analogy to illustrate the point. One could drive from Nottingham to London in a Rolls Royce or in a Trabant. The outcome would be the same (arrival in London) but the experience of travel would be qualitatively different. Of course a Trabant costs a lot less than a Rolls Royce. Outcome measures could therefore actually be equated with economy, effectiveness or efficiency rather than quality.

A focus on outcome measures could also serve to hide any quality loss in the service process brought about by resource constraints. Consider another analogy. In terms of a General Practitioner's (GPs) practice the '3 E's' may call for the GP to spend as little time as possible with each patient - only sufficient to diagnose and prescribe or make referral. This would mean that he/she can see as many patients as possible over the course of the day. But the quality of service delivery as perceived by the patient would necessitate a personal touch - which would mean more time spent with each patient and consequently lower throughput. An interesting twist is that if is there is a significant placebo effect a high throughput and low satisfaction might lead to a smaller health gain than a slower pace. A concern with the '3 E's' and outcome would be interested in total health gain of the locality which would be achieved with high throughput of patients. Of course the best service would be the one which got the balance right between the personal touch and throughput. The point though, is that there is likely to be a trade-off between the '3 E's' and quality.

However, government and employers in the UK are focussing upon outcome in order to monitor services (particularly in relation to contracting in a mixed economy of service provision). The outcomes are, moreover, generally comparative - e.g. comparative number of operations performed; comparative size of waiting list; comparative cost per operation etc. This emphasis on outcome has led to the development of outcome scales for publicly financed services - such as those in the Health of the Nation initiative.

Outcome Scales

Health of the Nation Outcome Scales (HoNOS) have been developed for every part of Health care, but a focus upon the scale for severe mental illness (which also has relevance for social services) illustrates the way these work. Three targets for the improvement of mental health in the UK are set out in the Government's Health of the Nation Strategy which was first launched in 1992. The first of these is a broad aim:

To improve significantly the health and social functioning of mentally ill people.
(Department of Health, 1994, p.4)

The other two aims relate to the achievement of specified reductions in suicide rates. In order to address the first aim a means of measuring outcomes of interventions in mental health care settings was devised in order to express this target explicitly and to monitor the extent of its achievement. Outcome measures have now been piloted for every part of the National Health Service. Following three years of development and evaluations the Health of the Nation Outcome Scales for Severe Mental Illness (HoNOS-SMI) became available in the latter part of 1995. This has relevance for both health and social care professionals in this field.

The aim of HoNOS-SMI is to provide a brief, accurate and relevant measure of 'health and social outcome' and is to be used in routine clinical practice. There are 3 items for behaviour, 2 for impairment, 3 for symptoms and 4 for functioning in a social context. Each item is broken down into sub sections and rated on a 5-point scale. The idea is that outcome of interventions can be measured by comparing scores for the same individual over time. From this information, it is intended to set a national target in terms of increasing health and social functioning. This will be measured in large-scale aggregated data that will include change scores that demonstrate other kinds of desired outcomes such as the slowing of anticipated deterioration.

The Government hopes that the routine collection of outcome data will provide a means of expressing the first mental health target in a quantifiable way; and monitoring progress towards that target at local and national level. At the time of writing the exact means of achieving these aims have not yet been finalised, but it is possible that local comparisons may be made between groups receiving similar types of care, or coming from similar geographic sectors etc. There is a commitment that such comparisons should be made only under the supervision of a competent authority - such as an academic department. HoNOS are meant to complement, not replace existing quality assurance systems.

Changes in HoNOS ratings over time would provide data for case reviews. Similarly HoNOS are intended to be of use to purchasers in the contracting process by addressing questions of health gain and its measurement and by contributing to a more definitive estimation of that group of patients referred to as suffering from severe mental illness. The idea of HoNOS is that outcome of professional interventions can be measured by comparing scores for the same individual over time. These data will be aggregated and it is intended to set national targets in terms of increasing health and social functioning. On the face of it such a development seems unproblematic, but in reality can have severe consequences for the professions and their clients.

The Impact on Professional and Service Users

One of the difficulties for employers in introducing change in working practices has been the resistance of professional groups. Quality outcome targets linked with wider deregulation can be used to control professional activity in such a way as to allow managers to redefine the labour process. This is particularly the case if the state sets national targets for professional action. An example is the proposal announced by Michael Howard, the Home Secretary, that the pay of probation officers might be linked with their performance (Guardian 10.4.96). Under this scheme pay (or part of it) will be dependent upon the professional achieving national targets with his/her clients. In this case the pay of probation officers will suffer if their clients (or too many of them) commit crime whilst on probation. It does not take too great a leap of the imagination to envisage the same principle carried into other areas of professional activity (including nursing) once they have national targets to achieve.

Certainly it is significant that HoNOS is being forwarded by the Department of Health as a means of targeting and prioritising services. This is unfortunate as the scales actually provide only a crude indication of the condition of users. For example only client records over the two weeks prior to the client reviews are considered in the scale. It also raises the issue of the reliability of the data collected. If such pressures existed the scales would be open to possible manipulation as the client reviews could be timed so as to exclude, say, incidents of aggressive behaviour. Alternatively they could be used by clinicians to defend their services by illustrating that their clients need high resource input because of fluctuating or high HoNOS scores.

This also highlights a distinction between service outcomes and the processes by which outcomes are achieved. Professionals and service users are primarily concerned with quality of process (or service delivery), Measures such as HoNOS with outcome. A mix of measures of both process and outcome can complement one other. However, health and social care employers are increasingly focussing upon outcome in order to monitor service quality (particularly in relation to contracting in a mixed economy of service provision).

Parton (1994) has examined the ways in which outcome indicators has become a highly relevant part of management control of policy, practice and professionalism within and across welfare organisations. Although social work has not had the same sort of fundamental management review as health, Parton argues that similar accountability forces are in play:

> The increased emphasis on management, evaluation, monitoring, and constraining professionals to write things down, is itself a form of government of them, and more crucially, of those with whom they are working. It forces them to think about what they are doing and hence makes them accountable against certain norms. In the process power flows

59

to the centre or manager who determines the professionals' inscriptions, accumulates them, analyses them in their aggregate form and can compare and evaluate the activities of others who are entries in the chart.
(Parton, 1994, p.26)

Managers are now able to shape the labour process and this has allowed them to define what it is that determines quality in services. Professionals have an absolute concept of quality of practice and service which is a part of their professional value system. Managerial concepts of quality may be more interwoven with organisational concerns.

Power has shifted to the managers and away from the professionals. There are many on both the political left and right who would applaud this. Professionals are viewed in some quarters as welfare bureaucrats who hold a vested interest in retaining a place in the planning and assessment of services (Audit Commission, 1992). It is interesting that the Audit Commission did not also view managers in the same light.

New Public Management Reform

Pollitt (1995, pp.133-154) lists the elements of New Public Management (NPM) as:

- Cost cutting, capping budgets and seeking greater transparency in resource allocation.
- Desegregating traditional bureaucratic organisations into agencies often related to the parent by a contract of quasi contract.
- Decentralisation of management authority *within* public agencies (flatter hierarchies).
- A separation of the function of providing public services from that of purchasing them.
- Introducing market and quasi-market mechanisms.
- Requiring staff to work to performance targets, indicators and output objectives (performance management).
- Shifting the basis of public employment from permanency and standard national pay and conditions towards term contracts, performance related pay and local determination of pay and conditions.
- Increasing emphasis on service 'quality', standard setting and 'customer responsiveness'.

In the UK the process of desegregating central departments into core functions and executive agencies had, by 1995, produced a situation in which 63 percent of all civil servants were working in agencies and NPM had been introduced in almost every part of the public sector in some shape or other (Chancellor of the Duchy of Lancaster, 1994). Given the scale and significance of these and other changes it might be supposed that New Public Management (NPM) would have attracted a great deal of evaluation particularly as 'some of the techniques which make up the NPM's armamentarium lay great stress on evaluation as a means of "closing the feedback loop"'. (Pollitt, 1995, p.135). However, NPM reforms have generally occurred and remained without fundamental evaluation as to its worth. In particular NPM creates a tension between cost cutting and down sizing on the one hand, and on the other quality improvement. NPM seems to be far more closely associated with cost reductions rather than service improvements. For example in Trosa's work examining the UK's Next Steps reforms this argument is forwarded:

> ...even if agencies have different kinds of targets, financial (productivity), efficiency and quality, the enquiry shows that financial targets are given a much higher priority.
> (Trosa, 1994, p.9)

This is supported in research by Talbot's work *Reinventing Public Management*, (1994) who found that the need to reduce costs was the single most important driving force behind NPM changes. Pollitt (1995) raises the question of whether any productivity increases are the result of new public management or the response organisations tend to make anyway when faced with reduced budgets. This is a question which remains largely unexplored. However, Donald Light in his study of the UK National Health Service argued that the introduction of NPM and market reforms actually *increased* inefficiencies, largely because the transaction costs and market failures involved in the running of the quasi-market outweighed any benefits gained by efficiency savings (Light, 1997). This is not a new argument, Scheffler previously argued 'There is little doubt that the NHS reforms will increase the percentage of GNP spent on health care' (Scheffler, 1992, p.183). Also Hughes observed that 'the most salient lesson of all from the US is that transaction costs soar in a developed market system...' (1995, p.292). This is largely a 'rediscovered' area of economics, but earlier thinking in economics has argued that competition is ill suited to health care (cf. Samuelson, 1955; Boulding 1958). The arguments are summarised by Light:

> Health care is often *emergent* as diagnosis and treatment unfold. Clinical decisions are *contingent* on what is found and how the patient reacts. Cases are highly *variable* and the course of treatment uncertain. These qualities mean that no clear product, with clear property rights, can be defined and its price set, as can be done for hotel rooms or computers. Put another way, health care has a large grey area in which

61

services and products can be manipulated by the provider/seller, or by a contractor of services, so as to appear cheaper by treating less illness or by treating illness less. (Light, 1997, p. 299)

The same could be said of much of the public services. Indeed, management journals are filled with the problems of managing costs in a market and how to reduce demand. Mark and Brennan rediscovered the term 'demarketing' and illustrated ways in which this concept could be utilised. They define demarketing as '...that aspect of marketing that deals with discouraging customers in general or a certain class of customers in particular on either a temporary or permanent basis' (1995, p.18).

Such developments have led to professional concerns that standard setting by professions should not be subject to outside review or managerial control. This inevitably leads to conflict with the management ethos. Flynn has examined this potential conflict between managerialist and professional approaches and provided an analysis based upon conflicting value systems. See figure 6.

In Flynn's quadrant 1, where managers dominate and the culture is inward looking, the result is an organisation obsessed with budgets and procedures, with little time for service users. In quadrant 2, the professionals have control, but are more concerned with their own standards than the needs of their clients. Quadrant 3 would be represented by professionals who set their own standards, but take into account the needs of their clients. An example, used by Flynn, is of schools who try to guarantee employment for their leaving pupils. In quadrant 4, where organisational control is by managers, but which is also outward looking towards the needs of service consumers, is the ideal sought under many public sector reforms. However, as Flynn goes on to point out, this managerial model highlights the fundamental difference between the private and public sectors:

> If businesses are outward looking and consumer oriented, they generate sales which produce revenue. (And)... It is possible to make public services more user oriented through careful service design. But what if that effort produces greater expectations and more demand for services? A rationing process has to take place, unless there is an open- ended budget. Competition between individual units may create extra revenues for those units which are successful, but the total budget is still fixed. Once there is rationing combined with public accountability, there is need for judgement. Professional and political judgements about who is entitled to what and who can benefit from what are quite different from judgements about what will sell.
>
> This crucial difference, the fact that there is no 'sale' connecting the organisation to its users in the way companies

**Figure 6: Conflict Between Managerial and
Professional Approaches**

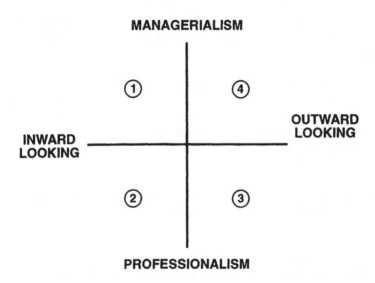

are connected to their customers, means that the wholesale importation of private sector management techniques and ideologies that go with them is inappropriate. (Flynn, 1990)

A not dissimilar view has been proffered by Drucker who argues that in commercial organisations the fundamental objective of the organisation should be maximising profit, whilst in the public sector organisations the concern should be in using resources to change people, making them healthier, wiser etc. (Drucker, 1991). Parsons also generally supports this view, arguing that the difference between what he terms 'the managerial bottom line' in the public and private sectors is fundamental:

> Managers in the public sector manage for social result, with resources as means; private sector managers use social objectives as a means to economic results. This is not a difference in management tasks necessarily, but a difference in why those tasks are undertaken and in how they are done. (Parsons, 1964, p.34)

Parsons goes on to argue that the recent reforms in the public sector have missed this crucial difference by focussing primarily upon efficiency and value for money:

> The consequence has been that little time has been given in the process of reform to defining what values public money is meant to produce and thus to what results managers are to be held to account. Without that definition of expected result, the proposition of 'value for money' reduces to a simple concern for cheapness and many implicitly intended values are in danger of being lost. (Parsons, 1964, p.35)

A number of commentators are now arguing that public sector management needs to develop in ways which are appropriate to the management of public services. In the forefront of these discussions is Flynn's view that public sector management needs to be built around '...the analogous relationship between the organisation and its users' (Flynn, 1990). This would involve building up appropriate forms of producer-consumer exchange which enhances the moral of the producers and the respect they have for the task (public service ethic) and providing services which can be flexible in meeting changing demands.

This raises a concern for evaluation. Evaluators are often asked to evaluate services within accepted and taken frameworks, that evaluation be apolitical. However, this can be problematic and evaluators rarely recommend the deconstruction of service organisation because it moves them from the realm of evaluation and into politics. For example, the rise in the numbers of managers in the NHS over recent years has certainly become a concern for government - but only very recently evaluators. The difference perhaps is that professionals have been associated with the public service ethic (effectiveness?), managers with achieving efficiency (Page, 1995) which was the political direction - perhaps this is why they have withstood close scrutiny of their activities for so long.

Regardless of the problems with NPM and the subsequent focus on outcomes, there is also an argument that it is outcome which should be the most important part of public service evaluation - not the way that the outcome was achieved. After all a nation only has so much that it can spend on welfare so the maximisation of those welfare pounds should be a fundamental aim of a responsible management and a responsible government. This is a strong argument. However, the way in which outcome measurement is used to establish quality in welfare services raises a number of issues - not least for evaluation practice.

Citizens Charter

In order to determine outcomes the focus of attention has moved towards identifying elements of a service which can be easily monitored and where standards can be established. This is in line with NPM principles. A part of this approach has been the development of citizens' charters. The first of these charters in Europe was the UK Citizens Charter which was introduced in 1991. This was closely followed in 1992 by the French Chartes de Services Publics and the Belgian Charte de l'Utilisateur des Services Publiques. These charters all differ slightly in terms of legal standing but are broadly the same concept for the same end. The purpose is to specify in advance service targets which must be met - such as the length of time one has to wait for a service. This macro approach also utilises audit and inspection as a monitor of service effectiveness and quality. The aim is to express targets in a quantifiable way which are visible for service purchasers (government) and citizens.

However, the managerial dominance of evaluation, with its emphasis on demonstrating outcomes and its involvement in continuing funding encourages services to report that outcome targets have been achieved. One example of this is the evaluation of Accident and Emergency (A & E) Units in the UK against Citizens Charter stipulations. The Citizens Charter stated that all patients would be assessed within five minutes of entering A & E. This initially caused problems for hospitals with only a very small percentage of units making the grade. However, the managerial response was to have a 'triage nurse' assess a patient on entry to the unit. The length of time that patient may then have to wait for treatment is not assessed by Citizens Charter. Another example is that of operation waiting lists. The Citizens Charter specifies maximum waiting list times for operations. However, a NHS Trust may respond to this by placing patients on 'consultant review'. Here the patient is seen on a regular basis by the consultant to see if they need to go onto the operation waiting list. In other words a hidden waiting list has emerged to get onto the official waiting list. The concern arises whether people may ever get treatment if they are not on the official list. What is more, there is a concern that the actual service need is becoming hidden from view. A similar situation exists in Social Services. Social Services have to assess the need of all presenting clients. However, with tight budget constraints there is concern that existing availability of service will determine which needs are acknowledged. This is not a new issue for Local Authorities. There is an analogy with the Education Act of 1981, which introduced 'statementing' to identify special educational needs. There is a general belief that local education authorities have often attempted to statement on the basis of service availability rather than need (Page, *et al.*, 1994).

The issue of unmet and hidden need has been taken up by the House of Commons select committee on health:

> ...it will be difficult to judge in the future whether resources
> are adequate unless we have a clear identification of the level
> of need - both met and unmet.
> (Craig, 1993, p.12)

The reporting of success is important and organisations tend to find ways of adapting a minimalist approach to meeting quality hurdles. Given the pressure on state resources and massive social and economic problems an evaluation which was critical of a service, or critical of its impact on the quality of life of its recipients against the larger context of social and economic disadvantage, would probably bring an end to the programme being evaluated. This raises issues of the credibility of in-house evaluations and also performance claims against macro instruments such as Citizens Charter and HoNOS.

Issues in Service Evaluation

Several issues arise from this work. First, there is a concern that evaluation by outcome measures and performance indicators may hide quality loss in the service. What is more, it may not be impossible for a service to perform well against such measures but actually be engaging in activities which do not further the organisations core aims. The lack of publicly stated goals for both health and social care mean that there will be competing sets of goals (or theories about the service) held by the different stakeholders - but that does not mean that an evaluation on the basis of goals should not be attempted.

Evaluation by comparison and by league table (particularly where resources are linked to where one is in the league) is a notion of competition borrowed from the private sector. However, such notions are not wholly conducive to the welfare sector. Firstly, there is no (or even an adverse) incentive for organisations doing well on league table criteria to share the basis of their success with other organisations who may be doing less well. Although an imperative exists the speed of organisational learning may consequently be affected. But even if organisations did readily share information on success this would not necessarily mean that what works well for one organisation would also work well for another. This hits a key issue. The logic behind outcome measures and league tables is that the same intervention should always produce the same result. If it does not, the reason must lie in the quality of intervention. This reasoning is based upon a problematic view of experimental logic. It is problematic because it is a misreading of the goals and aims of the natural sciences. Even universal laws on cause and effect are not always true. Universal laws in the natural sciences are ones which are always present *in the conditions specified* (Pawson & Tilley, 1997).

The evaluation of services needs to go beyond performance indicators, outcome measures, quality circles, user satisfaction questionnaires etc to contribute towards policy and service development. This necessitates a knowledge about and understanding of user's lives. A focus on cause and effect requires that the context is irrelevant and that it should be stripped away from analysis. But in health and social services it is often the different contexts which shape and alter meanings. Evaluation on the basis of outcome or performance generally does not ask the key questions 'Does this service work; how does it work; why does it work; could it work better another way?'. In other words there is an argument that Evaluation should match the outcomes to identified mechanisms (which create outcomes from interventions) and the context (social, political and economic). This would also be one way to address the issues raised from organisational theory.

Decontextualised and Depoliticised Evaluation

An emphasis on outcome and performance related evaluation serves to decontextualise and depoliticise services. It is, of course, only proper that health and social services, however provided, are required to demonstrate the ways in which their funding has been used and with what effects - either as a condition of the funding contract or in order to secure further monies. However to evaluate services without taking account of the context of that service assumes that the service is a variable on its own which can be separated for study. This is an atheoretical approach which serves to depoliticise welfare services which are, after all, constructed within legislative, policy and funding processes and shaped through dimensions of inequality. To assume that services exist outside of these processes usually means the acceptance of a 'taken for granted' perception of services:

...the political relationship between taken for granted understandings and dominant ways of seeing things in a society divided by gender, race, class, sexuality disability and age should make us extremely wary of evaluations that focus only on the practice as though it existed uncontentiously within a policy and social vacuum.
(Everitt, 1996, p.174)

Health and social services, through their work, develop understanding of the effects of social and economic policies upon people's lives. An important part of policy development should be to make known such knowledge and the way in which policies and services may impact upon disadvantage and inequality. An evaluation that is decontextualised and scrutinizes services as a separate entity not only fails to provide opportunities for learning of the effects of discriminatory social and economic policies, but also may do just the opposite and serve to support these (Everitt, 1996).

Current modes of evaluation do not question, and in fact actually support the pursuit of economy and efficiency - and that may well be why they are in place. Changing the emphasis to evaluate against progress towards organisational goals would place a regulatory framework over pursuit of economy and efficiency as it may then be possible to gauge the extent to which resource constraints hinder goal achievement.

4 Issues Arising from the Commissioning of Research: Case Studies

Case Study 1: Evaluating the Transferability of Nursing Skills

The commissioning of Public Service research became influenced by the public sectors drive towards the '3 E's' from the mid 1980s. In short, research commissioners became primarily concerned with what service outputs are we getting for our resource inputs. The issues of such a simple causal basis for research has been addressed in Chapter 1. What follows is a case study report of a research project funded by the Department of Health in 1990. This project has not previously been publicly reported and so the methodological strategy is outlined in some depth here. This was a 2-year project, on which I worked and which examined the transferability of the skills of the registered mental handicap nurse (RNMH) from hospital to community settings. The key question was whether nurses could be transferred straight into community settings without retraining. A brief examination of the policy background is required to understand the key issues.

A Brief Policy Background

In the early 1970s, initially following public outrage over the maltreatment of patients and the conditions highlighted in the Report of the committee of enquiry into Ely Hospital Cardiff, 1969 (which was reinforced by a series of hospital enquiries elsewhere in the UK) community care for people with a learning disability gained a place upon the government's policy agenda. However, one of the major problems involved in moving people with learning disability out of hospital and into the community was that the overwhelming majority of staff who were trained to care for the client group were nurses then trained predominantly in a medical ideology. DHSS statistics for England indicated that in 1977 there were only 1,907 whole time equivalent numbers (wte) staff employed in local authority community homes for people with a learning disability compared with 24,515 wte nurses engaged in the care of the learning disabled in hospital. A report by the Audit commission in 1988 and the White Paper 'Caring for People' charted a policy of transferring responsibility to social services. However, even in 1990 although the balance had changed over the years since 1977 most of the staff trained to care for this client group were still located in the health services.

Also in response to the changing locus of care (in communities), the mental handicap nursing bodies had changed their training to fully encompass the 'social elements of care'. This also incorporated moving the majority of their training into community settings. This training was internationally recognised as for its excellence (Shaw, 1994). The question which faced government as the responsibility of services changes was whether there was a future for the RNMH qualification. Were the nursing skills utilised transferable across settings and how did their skills compare to those staff with other qualifications, and none? This was the question to be addressed by the research.

The project methodology was in two stages. The first stage involved a postal survey of every District Health Authority and Social Service Department in England to ascertain their professional skill mix, and other information including whether nurses were employed and in what capacity. The second stage, having received and analysed the survey responses, was to choose two areas which indicated that nurses were being assimilated into social services in a number of different settings. Once the two case study areas were identified the next task was to develop a methodology to evaluate the contribution of those with the mental handicap nursing qualification compare to those with alternative qualifications (such as the Certificate in Social Care (CSS)) and people with no qualifications. Apart from interview and non-participant observation data (which ultimately proved critical) the research team were also faced with the need to develop a quantitative tool in order to carry out the evaluation, as commissioned.

Two criteria were required of methodology to achieve such an end. It had to be flexible enough to be of use in relation to the different groups of staff and it had to be amenable for use by staff who did not have professional qualifications in care. The original intention was to take such a measure 'off the shelf', but on closer investigation it was found that existing instruments would not meet our purpose. As a consequence a new instrument called the Staff Activity Checklist (SAC) was developed. Ideas and principles were taken from established material but adapted and extended to meet the specific needs of the research project.

This new checklist moved away from time-sampling methodology to real-time and away from the use of pen and paper to hand held computers. At the time of the research, 1990, this was innovative. The SAC generated data which enabled the evaluation of the contributions of staff with varying professional backgrounds and none on the basis of the following simple model:

- the input (training)
- the output (activities)
- and one aspect of the outcome (quality of intervention)

The validity of the new measure was established using various procedures including arranging for the research team to observe staff activities in a pilot study location whilst themselves being observed by two national figures from the mental handicap nursing profession (a sort of them watching us watching you). The result of this process was the SAC which broke down mental handicap care activity into 22 separate core activities under four broad headings. For interest the SAC is detailed below:

The Staff Activity Checklist

- Contact with Clients
   i)   self-care: supervise/do with client(s)/ instruct client(s) to do
   ii) self-care: physically assist client(s) to do
   iii) self-care: do the task for the client(s)
   iv) self-care: (unobserved - such as toileting)
   v)   educational/training activities with client(s)
   vi) clinical care
   vii) responding to challenging behaviour
   viii)sharing active leisure activity with client(s)
   ix) communication: verbal
   x)   communication: sign language
   xi) communication: other
   xii) other contact with client(s)

- Contact with Informal Carers
   xiii) contact with relatives/informal Carers, education or training
   xiv)   other contact with informal Carers

- Management and Supervision
   xv)   management/administration relating to individual clients
   xvi)   staff or unit management
   xvii) staff training and supervision
   xviii) staff interaction - other
   xix)   other management activities

- Other Activities
   xx)   home or unit 'housekeeping' tasks
   xxi) linking/waiting
   xxii) other/unobserved

The project team then developed a computer analysis package by which they could log these activities in relation to time. In the end the team had a tool with which to undertake a complex sort of time and motion study using hand held computers. Having achieved this the new methodology was tested to establish inter-rater and system reliability. The project researchers then spent three months following nursing and other care staff around (tracking) and logging their activities on the SAC. Staff were tracked in a number of settings and with variable degrees of professional skill mix - day care, small community homes, hostels, community teams etc. The data was then downloaded to a mainframe for analysis using spss. The whole project took two years and frequent progress reports were dispatched to the Department of Heath. What was found in the end?

An analysis of variance of activities engaged by all professional staff between each service setting showed *no* significant differences in their degree of engagement in each of the activities logged on the SAC. An analysis of variance was then carried out between the activities for the staff groups (RNMH, other qualified and unqualified) within agencies (voluntary sector, health, social services) and again no significant differences were discovered between the activities of the staff as logged onto the SAC. An analysis was then undertaken between the activities of the staff groups of all observed staff regardless of setting to see if there was any overall significant differences. Yet again none emerged.

It is worth examining the overall picture which emerged from this evaluation which are set out in diagrams 1, 2 and 3. Here the categories from the original checklist are grouped together under the four main headings. From the first pie-chart we can see that the most of an RNMH's time (45 percent) is spent on management and training activities, 35 percent is spent on other direct care, 18 percent on supporting self care and 2 percent of their time is spent with informal Carers. When this is compared with the pie-chart which outlines the breakdown for other qualified staff we see little difference: 50 percent on management/training; 33 percent on other direct care; 15 percent on promoting self care; 2 percent on contact with informal Carers. The implication from this is that expensive to train RNMH staff are doing much the same activities as less expensively trained Enrolled Nurses or those with the CSS qualification. However, when we contrast these two charts with the activities of staff with no professional qualifications some differences can be seen - though these differences were not statistically significant.

Perhaps the most interesting point is that staff with no professional qualifications had the highest contact time with clients. Also when the different groups of qualified staff were asked subjectively, in interview, to rate their

Diagram 1: RNMH Qualified Staff

percentage of time spent on activities

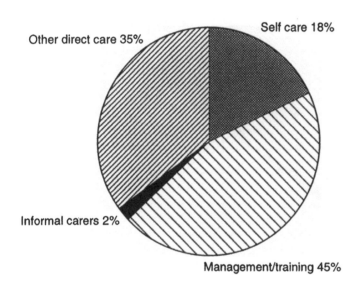

Other direct care 35%

Self care 18%

Informal carers 2%

Management/training 45%

Diagram 2: Other Qualified Staff

percentage of time spent on activities

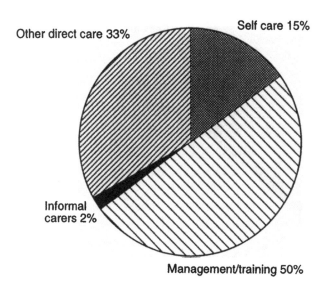

Other direct care 33%

Self care 15%

Informal
carers 2%

Management/training 50%

Diagram 3: Unqualified Staff

percentage of time spent on activities

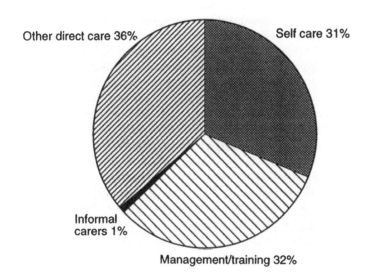

Other direct care 36%

Self care 31%

Informal
carers 1%

Management/training 32%

utilisation of the activities listed under the SAC headings the results were very similar to the statistical picture which subsequently emerged. Also when the variable 'quality of interaction with clients' was examined, there was, again, a very similar picture across the qualification groups and no statistically significant differences were found.

One implication from this research is that expensive to train qualified staff are not needed for this client group - non-professionally qualified staff will do the job just as well. But is this really the case? Another argument could be that, although the project team demonstrated that the SAC measure had been well tested, it was new, and therefor the reliability of the measure was unknown. However, having read the previous chapters one will possibly realise that neither of the above alternatives capture the reality of the situation. Indeed, the project team were aware that this finding was a possibility before the project started.

The research criteria specified that the strategy was to try and evaluate the contributions of staff with varying professional backgrounds, and none, on the basis of a simple causal model which related training inputs to activity outputs across different settings, and tried to see if outputs varied. The use of quantitative methodology was also specified. This is becoming increasingly common within government projects and there is often a hierarchy of methodology involved in evaluating projects at the commissioning stage, with experimental methodology at the top and qualitative methodology at the bottom (as in the Department of Healths 'York' model). However, having a hierarchy of method does not mean a hierarchy of argument or quality in research and realistically the Department of Health commissioned far too simple a model. There are complex social processes involved in the day to day interaction of staff and clients in the services. A 'methodologically sound' evaluation would require a research model with a different focus. As a minimum the focus would not be upon inputs and outputs, but rather on understanding the *processes* whereby inputs are turned into outputs. This would attempt to connect the training to the activity.

However, the project team also observed the staff activity as they were logging it and came to their own judgements about some of the processes involved. In particular that the activities of staff without professional qualification were largely the result of encouragement, training and support by the RNMH qualified staff. When those qualified staff were not there care became slightly more mechanistic (but not enough to register on the quality scale used). The argument raised here is that the presence of qualified staff not only maintained quality of care but also RNMH (and sometimes other qualified) staff provide a structure of support which they both created and maintained. Staff without professional qualification could engage in a broad range of activities confident in the knowledge that if a problem arose support was at hand.

Where the quantitative data suggests no significant difference, the qualitative data suggested that part of the 'output' of RNMH qualified staff is to 'bring up' the quality of activity of other Carers close to those of their own. Hence no significant differences were found when measured against the SAC. What is more, the dominant model of care found was based around what has become known as 'the nursing process'. Put simply this moves away from hierarchy and requires the person who finds a 'problem' to deal with it themselves, regardless of how highly they are qualified.

This raises the question that if the research team was aware of this possibility before the project started why did they go ahead and undertake all the work? There are several reasons for this. First, it should be acknowledged that academics are themselves assessed against periodic research assessment exercises. There have been recent examples of academics being 'retired' very early if they do not do well against the assessment criteria. Securing research grants is one way to ensure a good assessment. Also promotion of academics is increasingly linked to research performance. As a consequence, the opportunity to secure a research projects is not lightly turned down. However, another reason is that if the project team actually told the funders their suspicions, and asked for resources to examine mechanisms, the funders may have been cynical of their motives and may have given the research elsewhere - perhaps to a team which did not understand the importance of the small qualitative element in the project. Also the criteria of research is usually set by commissioning bodies after long consultation and it is usually not open to negotiation. This team knew that they could emphasise the qualitative evidence in their findings in order to illustrate the point. There was also, of course, the possibility that having convinced the funders that their research criteria was flawed they may have the opportunity to secure subsequent research which would focus upon appropriate criteria. Although this seems to support the view that researchers should bring their own preferences into evaluations, and it should be recognised that these are difficult to exclude at the best of times, it also raises the question - can/do research commissioners specify research criteria in order to achieve findings likely to be desirable to them?

Case Study 2: Evaluating Mental Health Services

Much of the concepts discussed in this case study are a product of initial work which was undertaken by the author and Hugh Middleton, Division of Psychiatry University of Nottingham, to develop a framework to evaluate the UK's Mental Health Act Commission (MHAC). This framework was not subsequently adopted because the parameters of the evaluation changed to examine only the data collected by MHAC. This research is ongoing at the time of writing.

> The basis of this framework is the idea, postulated by Scheid and Greenley, that '...organisations are deemed successful by their constituents when they conform to institutional demands and expectations that are both internally and externally generated.
> (Scheid and Greenley, 1997, p.403)

The increasing rationalisation of health care has brought the focus of managers and service purchasers upon the effectiveness and the efficiency of services and upon attempts to establish measurable outcomes. Indeed rationality desires quantifiable and measurable activities which can be laid open to evaluation. However, many parts of the health service, as discussed in an earlier chapter, do not sit well with such a rational model. Where this occurs an institutional model of organisational behaviour may provide a better basis for analysis (Hasenfeld, 1992) as the technical activities and processes of care are not tightly coupled to organisational outcomes. This makes the evaluation of organisational outcomes difficult, especially when there may be a wide range of opinions over the benefits of various treatments and intervention strategies.

Work within psychiatry has adapted medical models, or modifications of them and evaluations tend to follow suit. The experimental drug-trial epitomises this approach to evaluation. However, a growing body of literature has shown its inadequacy when used to look at complex behavioural phenomena. Much of the, discussion revolves around the point that previously accepted models and methods of research have not resulted in the answers sought in relation to the effect of a wide variety of change induction techniques. Perhaps one of the most general concerns has been the question of the relationship between outcome studies (of the results of 'treatment') and studies of process (what happens in 'treatment'). Much earlier work can be classified as either one or the other. But Chen (1990) has pointed out that this opposition of outcome and process studies is misguided. Pawson & Tilley (1997) argued strongly against 'spot the winner' type studies, but found that on considering the processes that might affect outcome that it is difficult to isolate any clear causal factors. The dilemma is that unless the change-inducing techniques can be described in sufficient detail to reproduce them, then the knowledge that some unknown thing is effective is not very useful. On the other hand taking 'flight into process' (Pawson, 1996) will not answer the question of whether this technique works or not in the hands of a sample of therapists. Thus, Shaw (1992) argues for a balance between process studies, and a complementary assessment of outcome, if real evaluation is to be achieved. The dichotomy between outcome and process studies has arisen from the way in which questions of evaluation are posed. The single question 'Does it work?' is meaningless, unless divided into a series of smaller core specific questions which can be looked at in turn. More recently, Shaw (1998) argues for specific interventions for specific problems with specific outcomes. Thus what may be improvement for one patient (relief from depression) may not be for another. In the same way, Tilley (1996) advises the avoidance of more formal evaluation designs. In particular mental health services can be evaluated against the extent to which they conform to normative beliefs and societal preferences which exist in the institutional environment.

It has been argued that evaluations of an organisations effectiveness involve 'explicit or implicit moral choices that are embedded in the practices ideologies'

(Hasenfeld (1992, pp.13-14) of service providers. Practice ideologies are concerned about belief systems as to what is good for the client.

The efficacy of and effectiveness of services are measured in light of these beliefs. In other words, mental health services are seen as effective if they are providing services that mental health care practitioners consider necessary to mental health. Much of the literature on effectiveness of mental health services focus upon either the client or the wider service. However, services are fragmented and uncoordinated and difficult to integrate. Consequently alternative approaches to the evaluation of mental health services have been developed.

Traditionally, two major perspectives are evident from the literature on organisational effectiveness. This is the systems approach and the goal approach. The systems approach is closely associated with the work of Yuchmann and Seashore (1967) and is based upon a systems model of organisational activity which emphasises the relationship between the organisation and the environment in which it operates. They argue that effectiveness is the degree to which an organisation can adapt to a changing environment and survive and that evaluating effectiveness will involve explicit or implicit value judgements with regards to what is of benefit to service recipients.

The goals approach sees organisations as rational and organised in such a way as to achieve goals. As a result effectiveness is arrived at by establishing the extent to which the organisation achieves its goals. This is the model behind the emphasis upon clinical audit and assessment. However, there is an empirical problem in establishing goals as an organisation may have many goals, the importance of each changing over time or on some other basis and there is also a difference between long term aims and goals which need to be accounted for. As a consequence, the goal model is best suited to those organisations where activity is directed towards specific outputs and where effectiveness can be established by focussing attention towards efficiency in achieving given outputs. This model has less applicability with organisations which pursue multiple, non-complementary or intangible goals.

The systems model is based upon an approach which stresses the relationship between the organisation and its environment. Here effectiveness is the degree to which an organisation survives or thrives in its environmental context. Organisational flexibility becomes a core concern under this model. There are a number of theories utilised within this broad approach. Contingency theory is used to focus upon the extent to which organisational structure fit the demands of the task environment; configuration theory argues that organisations have internally consistent designs which will fit multiple contexts and the extent to which they fit those contexts will determine their success. In this respect 'contexts' refers to public and staff relations, quality indices etc. This model is most appropriately used upon organisations where environmental turbulence is high and the effectiveness of the organisational system may predetermine the effectiveness of organisational goals. This is relevant to mental health services. This is particularly the case with public services where organisational resources are not secured in the market but are determined by a range of political and social factors. In such a situation the organisation's effectiveness could be gauged by examining the extent to which it satisfies the multiple stakeholders of the service. A distinction is usually made here between political, internal and external stakeholders (such as clients or customers). Often under this approach the preferences of the stakeholders are used as a basis of evaluating the organisations effectiveness. A final theoretical approach under this model is institutional theory. Here the argument is that acquiring resources and surviving turbulent environments are manifestations of an organisations successful conformity to institutional demands (D'Aunno, 1991). In terms of mental health, policies such as deinstitutionalisation the constituents in the institutional environment demanded community based care (Scheid and Greenley, 1997), whereas subsequent reforms have emphasised the empowerment of clients. Current concerns in mental health services are bringing cost containment and effective control to the fore, reflecting the wider institutional environment. Moreover, and as already discussed, different institutional demands may result in multiple organisational goals and the production of services which may both conflict and compete with each other for scarce organisational resources. Moreover there is evidence that dominant interest groups come to the fore in the face of conflicting institutional demands and that their goals tend to be given preference (Montgomery and Oliver, 1996).

The important point here is that institutional theory suggests that organisations conform to institutional demands it is unclear which goals will be conformed to when institutional demands are contradictory. The models of organisational effectiveness discussed in this chapter may consequently not be conflicting approaches so much as representing the different aspects of organisational activity relevant to evaluation research. In particular professional norms and practices are a central feature of the organisational activity of health services and each profession has a unique view of the service a client should receive. The actual service provided may consequently be the result of a process of negotiation between the different groups and the clients themselves. Organisations in complex environments, such as mental health services, will tend to develop structures that satisfy the various pressures upon them and these pressures may change from location to location. In its search for legitimacy mental health services must at least appear to conform to a wide range of institutional demands, some of which are contradictory, and these rapidly change. Of particular concern to mental health services is the boundary between caring for patients and controlling the risk they pose to both themselves and others. These are potentially contradictory demands and the emphasis, particularly of late, has been constantly shifting. It is for this reason that Hasenfeld argues that mental health services experience 'a cyclical legitimacy crises' (1992, p.11) as the institutional demands come into open conflict.

One organisational strategy to deal with diverse institutional demands is to diversify the organisation's services and activities and in mental health we have seen a wide range of different professionals emerge to fill specialised roles and services. As a consequence the organisational structure becomes more complex which in turn can make goal achievement more difficult as there is greater opportunity for disagreement with the increased number of actors. This can lead to goal incongruence as different elements of the organisation follow goals which are most important to them. This may also be fostered by different professional identities as each strive to improve their status within the organisation. Certainly research has often found that staff group variables may have been more powerful than treatment orientation effects. When this is not the case, methodological comparison requires some method of controlling for differential inputs to the treatment situation. This becomes difficult with complex organisations and a solely quantitative approach is unable to capture sufficient information to explain the dynamics of organisational life and the impact it has upon patients.

For health work to maintain its legitimacy it must not only be clinically effective but also acceptable to its recipients. Clinical effectiveness focuses upon professionals being satisfied that they have done their best to respond to the needs *they* define in their patients. The clinical literature of the mental health professionals is sadly lacking on this issue. Studies of users' views of services has, for example, been largely absent from journals such as the *British Journal of Clinical Psychology*. This contrasts with major studies of users views sponsored by 'mental health' charities such as MIND (cf. Faulkner, 1997). This pattern of publication may suggest that users' views are not a research priority for 'mental health' professionals, or the awarding bodies which fund their research. For example, when the Medical Research Council set out its list of priorities of research into schizophrenia, the views of patients were almost completely ignored. At the top of their list of 10 priorities were items such as 'genetic investigations', but no item exploring users' views of either services or interventions.

The studies which have looked at users' views (Rogers *et al.*, 1993; Faulkner, 1997) have suggested the following main findings:

1. Users prefer community rather than hospital based interventions.
2. They appreciate being offered choices about types of intervention and their siting and complain that choices are currently inadequate.
3. They tend to prefer psychological to biological treatments.
4. They appreciate, but complain of rarely receiving, informed consent about their treatment.
5. They have a variety of perceptions, or lay beliefs, about the nature of mental distress which range wider than that provided by services. If a service professional holds a view about aetiology and treatment which is at odds with patients expectations, this may lead to disaffection and lead to problems with compliance and satisfaction of service.

Taking these main points together would suggest that the service philosophy of hospital-based regimes, dominated by physical treatments are generally out of sync with the preferences of people with mental health problems.

If clinicians have been slow to embrace an interest in user satisfaction in their research priorities, the same can not be said of service commissioners. It is now common for commissioners to conduct consultation exercises to gain users' views on services and service planning and to include these as part of their local needs assessment when developing their 'mental health' strategies. As a consequence, a tension may exist between the priorities of clinicians and those of service commissioners (and lay people).

One of the particular features of 'mental health' services is that they are constrained by legal and social expectations of their role, which tends to invalidate certain fundamental expectations of health services which have been enshrined in documents such as the *Patients Charter*. Potential indicators of service quality, such as providing options for recipients and respecting their freedom of choice are essentially preempted by the rules governing mental health services. Those residing in Therapeutic Communities form part of the, approximately, 8 percent of psychiatric patients which are detained compulsorily in the UK.

Szasz (1963) has gone so far as to argue that psychiatric patients will never be offered choice while therapeutic law exists to enforce detention and treatment. This highlights a contradiction about the conceptualisation of health services. In the UK, since *Working for Patients* and the market reforms patients have been regarded as consumers. However, if psychiatric patients can be compulsorily detained and treated then they can not be regarded as consumers who voluntarily express a need for a service. In such circumstance how may the 'quality of services' imposed on such people be judged? One possible answer would be to enhance the role of the Mental Health Act Commission, which currently check to see that services comply with the Mental Health Acts, into a quality assurance role. However, this does not detract from the main line of argument which is that mental health services are only legitimate if they have the support of users and that user views should be solicited in any meaningful evaluation of such services and regimes.

In the light of the above discussion, it can be seen that mental health services present particular characteristics with respect to research methodology: In particular, they are multi-dimensional, and research is often designed to investigate single dimensions and they have multiple goals, of which outcome is but one. These goals have changed and will continue to change. These factors militate very strongly against comparing the activity of organisations in a snap shot study. Manning, in analysis of Therapeutic Communities, argues that a more productive approach should be at four levels:

1. Comparing a number of mental health services, in order to use natural variations to suggest relationships between constituent variables (such as size, staff training, leadership, environmental context, organisational arrangements, length of use, etc.).

2. Studying individual aspects which go to make up the service; in other words, attempting to dissect the constituent parts to see how they work together, which are more effective, and why.

3. Studying natural fluctuations within the service over time to ascertain relationships between, for example, levels of tension and the age-distribution of patients.

4. Attempting to delineate more clearly the individual requirements of each patient so that the treatment can be more closely matched to needs.

Such an approach, of necessity does not follow orthodox experimental design, even though much evaluation in mental health services is commissioned with 'experimental methodology' as an expectation or specification.

5 The Politics of Evaluation

Traditional academic values held by many evaluators encourage a non-political approach to their research, that research should be above political considerations. However, evaluators of public services also want to influence government policy-making. The evidence from this work is that this is a difficult path to tread. The case study of the transferability of nursing skills research, in particular, illustrates that evaluators have to be fully aware of the political implication of research undertaken otherwise they run the risk of becoming pawns of a political game. An early review of the relationship between politics and research was undertaken by Sjoberg (1975). He suggests that social scientists fail to understand the political nature of research because they have:

> An unrealistic view of the research process... The conceptualisation of the scientific process as expressed in most treatise on social research makes it impossible to grapple with the political and ethical issues that arise, especially in the area of evaluation research.
> (Sjoberg, 1975, p.30)

Evaluators can often find it difficult to see beyond their own notions of logical and rational judgements about the research despite the political nature of evaluation research. The problem remains as Sjoberg stated it almost a quarter of a century ago. Evaluators need to integrate the political into evaluation practice and '...understanding social research as a social enterprise' (1975, p.30).

More recently Patton (1986) argued that evaluation was inherently political and attempted to map out the parameters of the issue. These arguments are summarised below. He argued that the political nature of evaluation stems from:

84

1.	The fact that people are involved in evaluation in itself makes it a political process. Social research as a social enterprise means that the values, perceptions and politics of everyone involved impinge on the evaluation process from inception to conclusion.

2.	The classification and categorisations involved in evaluation are themselves constructed through political process. The concepts, theories and methods of evaluation research are normative and value laden. The way in which an evaluation problem is stated necessarily includes value orientations and subjective perceptions about both the nature of social reality and what it is important to know about that reality. The categories and classifications systems used directly affect the nature of the data collected.

3.	Evaluations are based upon empirical data. Data always requires interpretation. Social science, generally, is an enterprise based, in part, on probability. The data from evaluation presents probabilities and patterns - not facts and conclusions. Interpretation is only partially a logical, deductive process; it is also a value-laden political process. Actions taken and decisions based upon such data are necessarily best guesses.

4.	Evaluation desires action and decisions from the product of its work. This makes it part of a political process. Any given programmatic action or decision is a result of multiple factors and influences. Evaluation findings are just one input into the complex system of organisational functioning. Weighting those inputs is a political activity.

5.	The fact that evaluation examines programmes and organisations makes it part of a political process. Organisations are decision-making systems and, as such, there are tensions between rational and political forces. As Silverman observed (1971, p.205) '...Rationality [of an organisation] is limited... By the existence of many preference orders within and organisation'. There is conflict both within and between organisations. Conflict occurs over the distribution of resources, status and power. One of the weapons employed in organisational conflict is information - evaluation generates information.

6.	The information generated by evaluation leads to knowledge. Knowledge reduces uncertainty which facilitates action and action is necessary to the accumulation of power.

While the role of information in decision making is not always obvious it often can make a difference. As Patton (1986, p.294) argued:

> Decision-making, of course, is a euphemism for the allocation
> of resources - money, position, authority etc. Thus, to the
> extent that information is an instrument, basis, or excuse for

changing power relationships within or among organisations, evaluation is a political activity.

This work has shown that evaluations can be manipulated either consciously or unconsciously by various stakeholders. This raises the question on whether there are times when one should not evaluate. From the programme manager or funders' point of view, evaluating a programme which is clearly beyond redemption may be seen as a waste of time and effort. However, from another stakeholders point of view, say the consumer, negative evaluations of programmes or products can be life saving, whereas positive evaluations may only provide modest opportunities (Scriven, 1997).

However, it is futile to engage in an argument about whether or not evaluation should be involved in politics. Evaluation is an inherently political process. The degree of politicalisation may vary, but is never absent. Cronbach goes so far as to argue that 'a theory of evaluation must be as much a theory of political interaction as it is a theory of how to determine facts (1980). This raises the question of how an evaluation model could be developed that gives stakeholders, particularly those without any power, a better chance to have their views heard. The stakeholder model was originally developed in the early 1980s in an attempt to break the dominance of the power of research commissioners in favour of the aims and contents of the evaluation. The benefit of a stakeholder model is that it represents a constructive attempt at achieving increased justice within the evaluation by giving different interest groups a chance to articulate their own concerns. In this way the stakeholder model could be seen as a way of legitimising evaluations and political power. There is also little doubt that politicians could also utilise a stakeholder model of evaluation (such as 4th Generation Evaluation) in order to avoid other kinds of evaluation methodology which may, for example, identify a goals problem with the programme. A number of Evaluators have discussed the relationship between evaluation and politics in their work.

The work of Chelimsky (1995) examines how evaluation can best be placed within a political framework by describing its link with the political process. The argument is that evaluation must change and develop in line with the political process. The implication is that new political circumstances in a country will create change in the framework used for evaluation theory and practice. Weiss (1987), on the other hand, places evaluation within a broader context and examines the inter-relationship between politics and evaluation. There is a recognition that the programmes being evaluated have been brought about by a political process and that they consequently have legislative sponsors and supporters and that administrative careers will be attached to them. Further, generated evaluation reports are fed into this political arena and become a part of the decision-making process. In this respect evaluation reports, though they make a claim to being independent and/or objective unavoidably take a political position. Weiss also points out that the interaction between evaluation and politics can be understood by examining the impact of evaluation reports upon the policy community. In particular Weiss refers to interest groups such as professional associations, unions etc. whose interest is not only in disseminating knowledge:

> Their interest lies in advancing their own cases. If they find supportive information in evaluations, they make those findings part of their argument.
> (Weiss, 1988, p.14)

Weiss also examines the ways in which politics can influence evaluations. He argues that 'negative' pressure may be exerted in ways that bias the scope of evaluation research, for example to press for unrealistic time frames or to seek to influence research findings. Political actors, of course, will also use evaluation results selectively or suppress the release of an evaluation report. On the other hand Weiss argues that politics can sometimes have beneficial influences. For example, political disagreements can serve as a stimuli for initiation and replication of evaluation studies and can also serve to make the results of evaluation more visible. Weiss's work also examined whether it was possible to protect evaluations from political influences which could limit a critical and broad examination of the matter in hand. The risk of interference from powerful stakeholder groups can be a threat to an independent and fair evaluation and he described five strategies for maintaining credibility within a political context:

1. Present a specification of a full scope of the issues. If possible, the study should be designed to address the range of questions addressed by all parties involved. However, the implication is that issues not covered should be clearly stated when reporting the evaluation findings.
2. Maintenance of continuous communication. The importance of keeping stakeholders aware of the progress of the study.
3. Formation of advisory groups that can help ensure that the study has an appropriate scope for addressing the major factors of current debate.
4. Include a clear statement of the study's limitations in the final report and in summaries.
5. Include non-technical statements of findings when reporting.

Karlsson (1996) argues that power in the evaluation process and the connection between evaluation and politics is also visible when considering which criteria should be used for selection and judgement of what should be evaluated in a programme evaluation and in meta evaluation. Karlsson's work in Sweden highlights the problems of fairness in an evaluation that is concerned with different criteria which can be connected with different stakeholder groups. This was raised in an evaluation of a programme for school age care services in Eskilstuna, an area of Sweden with 90,000 inhabitants. The programme involved

500 children and their parents. He identified the following criteria as being important to the different stakeholder groups:

- The most important criteria from the politicians' point of view were generally about the efficiency and the utility of the programme in economic terms.
- From the managerial perspective one of the most important criteria was the degree to which the programme could be controlled or directed.
- The professionals in the programme were concerned about establishing clear goals and guiding principles which could facilitate the realisation of the programme.
- Parents were primarily concerned that the personnel were of high quality, so that the children could receive security and care, and provide a good service.
- The children were concerned to have a good relationship with their classmates and to have a good range of activities. Also important was the ways in which adults regarded them, for example, with warmth and respect for their own choices whilst at the same time giving them security.

The evaluation problem here is which criteria should carry what weight or importance. One perspective on this is to apply Rawls' (1985) theory of justice, in particular his ideas on universal contract theory. Here, through rational consideration, it is possible to reach a tenable idea of which criteria should apply in order to judge what is fair. One criticism of this theory, put simply, is that it gives a too abstract and philosophical perspective to a practical problem. The communitarian view criticise Rawls' concept as it is not possible for an individual to rise above their own subjective intuitions of fairness and their own cultural roots. Another way to approach the problem would be to facilitate communication between the different points of view represented in an evaluation. This would involve negotiation between the stakeholders to reach some compromise on the criteria weighting. Strauss (1979) advocates this approach as a way of avoiding open conflict on evaluation reports. However, the strategy of negotiation also contains its own problems of relative articularness, power and resources.

Karlsson attempts to solve this dilemma with reference to Socratic dialogue where:

> ...it is not primarily a matter of defending one's own beliefs by criticising what other people believe. The essence is to become clear about oneself, ones knowledge, ignorance etc. together with other people.
> (Molander, 1990, p.235)

This may be possible within a Swedish context, where there is a large concensus on welfare and other public programmes, however, it would not be likely to benefit a society with large political, economic and social differences/inequalities such as exist in the United Kingdom.

The issue of hidden agendas is particularly problematic, though a theory driven approach can be extremely useful in policy evaluation. Let me put a radical idea to you:

> It is obvious that Health policy has to fail.
> (Osborne, 1997, p.186)

Let me put another radical idea. That Government is aware of this and is changing the 'concept' of health as a result.

A part of the Beveridge reforms in 1948 was the idea that it was the duty of government to secure the well-being of the population. This has developed over the years to the parallel idea that it is a right of the population to be provided with health and well-being. It is this which has created increasing demands for health services. However, it is impossible to institute a 'right to health'. There is a fundamental reason for this:

> Health, to have any meaning, must be posited as a biological concept, outside of the remit of any direct health policy. That is, health must be, at least in part, a matter of fate. Health - good health - cannot derive from a right; good and bad health, however crude or subtle the criteria used, are facts - physical states and mental states.
> (Foucault, 1988, p.170)

This is not to say that there can be no such thing as health policy, but only that health cannot be a direct aspect of citizenship - only an indirect one. Governments can at best provide the conditions - a medical staffing, a hospital system, procedures of public health, sanitary infrastructures, employment legislation etc. - that put different sections of the population on a more or less equal footing with regards to chances for health; and they can pay professionals to attempt to cure (where possible) diseases after they have occurred. But they can not guarantee health. The conceptualisation of health is also problematic: One could argue that health is not an absolute or determinate concept but an essentially indeterminate, relative and elastic concept. It is possible that even if we were to eradicate all known diseases - one will still not have an absolute concept of health. This is because with every new provision the very concept of health will widen and extend until even something as normal as death becomes perceived as a pathology, a form of ill-health. In other words each time government takes steps towards the target of achieving the concept of 'health', the concept escapes over the horizon leaving behind technical problems and arguments about resources (Osborne, 1997).

The new ideology which the government has adopted to try to address this is that of the 'new public health' where people are encouraged to rely less on the medical system and more upon themselves. We are at a point in time where medical care is broadly viewed by the citizenry as a right. There is a growing demand for the extension of entitlements as new technologies and medications are discovered: the demands and rationing of Viagra is a case in point. This is precisely the time we are being pressured to use the system less - NHS Direct is a manifestation of that and should be evaluated against less usage of primary care services. Governments across the western world are using neo-liberal approaches to try to modify people's expectations of health services and to side-track demands for guaranteed access. A new ideology is emerging to break the link between the provision of services and demands for health improvement. The value of service access is being replaced with a new preoccupation with controlling at-risk behaviours. At a time of cost crisis self- discipline has emerged as a popular theme. In lieu of rights and entitlements, individual responsibility and self help move to the centre of discussion.

Victor Fuchs, a noted health economist writes:

> Some future historian, in reviewing mid twentieth century social reform literature will note... a 'resolute refusal' to admit that individuals have responsibility for their own stress.
> (Fuchs, 1974, p.46)

Robert Whalen of the US Department of Health writes more explicitly:

> Unless we assume individual and moral responsibility for our own health, we will soon learn what a cruel and expensive hoax we have worked upon ourselves through our belief that more money spent on health care is the way to better health.
> (Whalen, 1977)

Knowles argues that the primary critical choice facing the individual is 'to change his personal habits or stop complaining. He can either remain the problem or become the solution to it: beneficent government can not and should not do it for him' (Knowles, 1977). The attack this poses upon welfare rights is explicit. However it does pose the question as to how to envisage a right to health care without balancing an individuals responsibility to remain healthy. This was taken to its radical extreme by John Knowles at a US conference on future directions in health care:

> The idea of individual responsibility has been submerged in individual rights to be guaranteed by the state and delivered by public institutions. The cost of sloth, gluttony, alcohol,

intemperance, reckless driving, sexual frenzy and smoking have now become a national not an individual responsibility and all justified as individual freedom. But one man's or woman's freedom is another's shackles in taxes and insurance premiums.

(Knowles, 1980)

Knowles seeks sanctions against at-risk behaviour in the form of refusal to treat such 'offenders' by the NHS. In its extreme form this would constitute a form of victim blaming. Although this would be unacceptable to many Europeans, there are elements of the approach which are attractive, even to social democratic governments. What is attractive about the approach is the abandonment of the quest for an absolute which would be 'health' and the substitution in its place of two utilisable features. The first is achievable targets - such as those contained in UK Governments 'The Health of the Nation' and 'Our Healthier Nation' strategy documents.

The second is the concept of responsibility. Not only are people made responsible for their own health, and potentially victimized if they are irresponsible, but also the principles of responsibility works as a force throughout the whole health care system. So managers are made responsible for managing services like a business, general practitioners for managing their budgets and their patients. Because health is not an absolute value government is constructing its own values - targets are met, performance is monitored, success and failure evaluated. In this respect evaluation, which looks at such approaches in terms of patient empowerment could be viewed as a tool of government ideology which acts to legitimize their own construction of 'health'.

In my view there is no real solution to the political issues, including hidden agendas and other pressures which exist within and around evaluation. Evaluators should be clear about the theoretical line they are applying to evaluations and to be honest about the limitations of their work. Seeking out hidden agendas and addressing them is important, though this can be difficult when government set the parameters for the evaluation, which often happens. Even stakeholders who are left on the 'short end' of an evaluation and who may contest the findings, could accept that the evaluation team strived to be as fair, open and equitable as possible. In many circumstances this is the best that can be achieved.

Bibliography

Audit Commission (1992) *Citizens Charter - Performance Indicators*, HMSO, London

Baron R. M. & Kenny D. A., (1986) 'The Moderator-Mediator Variable Distinction in Social Psychological Research: Conceptual, Strategic and Statistical Considerations', *Journal of Personality and Social Psychology*, Vol.51, No.6, pp.1173-1182

Beck U., (1992) *Risk Society: Towards a new modernity*, Sage, London

Becker H. S., Geer B., Hughes, E. C. & Strauss A., (1961) *Boys in White*, University of Chicago Press, Chicago

Benson J. K., (1977) 'Innovation and Crisis in Organisational Analysis', *Sociology Quarterly*, Vol.18, pp.5-18

Bouckaert G., (1997) 'Improving Performance Measurement', in Halachmi A., and Bouckaert G. (eds) *The Enduring Challenges in Public Management: Surviving and excelling in a changing world*, Jossey Bass, San Francisco

Boulding K. E., (1958) *Principles of Economic Policy*, Prentice Hall, Englewood Cliffs, NJ.

Chelimsky E., (1995) 'Where We Stand Today in the Practice of Evaluation', *Knowledge and Policy*, Vol.8, pp.8-19

Chen T .S. (1990) *Theory Driven Evaluation*, Sage, New York

Cochrane A., (1971) 'Effectiveness and Efficiency', in *Health and Disease: A reader*, Open University Press, Milton Keynes

Cohen D.A. & Rice J.C., (1995) 'A Parent-Targeted Intervention for Adolescent Substance Abuse Prevention: Lessons learned', *Evaluation Review*, Vol.19, No.2, pp.159-180

Craig G., (1993) *The Community Care Reforms and Local Government Change*, Social Research Paper 1, University of Humberside, Hull

Cronbach L., (1980) *Towards Reform of Programme Evaluation*, Jossey-Bass, San Francisco, CA

Crouch C., (1997) 'The Terms of the Neo-Liberal Consensus', *Political Quarterly*, Vol. 68, no.4

D'Aunno T., (1991) 'The Effectiveness of Human Service Organisations: A Comparison of Models', in Hasenfeld, Y., (ed) *Human Services as Complex Organisations*, Sage, Newbury Park, CA

Dean H. & Taylor-Gooby P., (1992) *Dependency Culture: The explosion of a myth*, Harvester Wheatsheaf, Hemel Hempstead

Denzin N. K., (1978) *The Research Act*, McGraw Hill, New York

Dingwall R., (1992) 'Don't Mind Him - He's from Barcelona', in Daly J., McDonald I. & Willis E., (eds) *Researching Health Care*, Routledge, London

Dingwall R. & Strong P., (1985) 'The Interactional Study of Organisations: A Critique and Reformulation', in *Urban Life*, Sage, Vol.15, No.2

Donabedian A., (1976) *Some Issues in Evaluating the Quality of Health Care*, ANA Publications, Kansas City

Drucker P., (1991) *Principles of Management*, Heinemann, London

Ehrenfeld D., (1981) *The Arrogance of Humanism*, Oxford University Press, Oxford,

Etzioni A., (1964) *Modern Organisations*, Prentice Hall, New York

Everitt C., (1996) 'Developing Critical Evaluation', *Evaluation*, Vol.2, No.2, pp.173-188

Faulkner R., (1997) *Knowing Our Own Minds*, Mental Health Foundation, London

Finch J., (1983) *Family Obligations and Social Change*, Open University Press, Milton Keynes

Flynn N., (1990) *Public Sector Management*, Harvester Wheatsheaf, London

Foucault M., (1988) 'On Problematization', *History of the Present*, Vol.4. (Spring)

Friedman M., (1962) *Capitalism and Freedom*, Sage, New York

Fuchs V., (1974) 'A Tale of Two States', in Conrad P., (ed) *The Sociology of Health and Illness: Critical perspectives*, St. Martins Press, New York

Georgiou P., (1973) 'The Goal Paradigm and Notes Towards a Counter Paradigm', *American Sociology Quarterly*, Vol.18, pp.291-310

Giarini O. & Stahel W., (1989) *The Limits to Certainty: Facing risks in the new service economy*, Kluwer, Dordrecht

Giddens A., (1970) *The Constitution of Society*, Polity Press, Cambridge

Giddens A., (1994) *Beyond Left and Right: The future of radical politics*, Polity Press, Cambridge

Glennerster H., (1993) *Paying for Welfare: Towards 2000*, Prentice Hall, London

Gough I., (1979) *The Political Economy of the Welfare State*, Macmillan, London

Gotzche E., (1989) 'Drug Evaluation: Issues and Practice', *Lancet*, Vol.15, pp.189-191

Guba Y. & Lincoln E., (1989) *Fourth Generation Evaluation*, Sage, New York

Hammersley M., (1992) *What's Wrong with Ethnography?*, Routledge, London

Hassard J., (1990) 'An Alternative to Paradigm Incommensurability in Organisational Theory', in Hassard J. & Pym D., (1980) *The Theory and Philosophy of Organisations*, Routledge, London

Hassard J. & Pym D., (1990) *The Theory and Philosophy of Organisations*, Routledge, London

Hassenfeld Y., (ed) (1992) *Human Services as Complex Organisations*, Sage, Newbury Park, CA

Hayek F., (1976) *Law Legislation and Liberty*, Routledge and Kegan Paul, London

Hills J. (1993) *The Future of Welfare: A guide to the debate*, Joseph Rowntree Foundation, York

Hills J. & Burchardt T., (1997) *Private Welfare Insurance and Social Security: Pushing the boundaries*, Layerthorpe, York Publishing Service

Hogwood B.W. & Gunn L.A., (1984) *Policy Analysis for the Real World*, Oxford University Press, Oxford

Karlsson O., (1996), 'A Critical Dialogue in Evaluation: How Can the Interaction between Evaluation and Politics be Tackled?', *Evaluation*, Vol.2, No.4 pp.405-416

Knowles J.H., (1977) 'The Responsible Individual and Health', in Conrad P., (ed) *The Sociology of Health and Illness: Critical perspectives*, St. Martins Press, New York

Light D., (1997) 'From Managed Competition to Managed Cooperation: Theory and Lessons from the British Experience', Seminar paper presented at University of Nottingham

Lindesmith A. E., (1947) *Opiate Addiction*, Principia Press, Bloomington, IN

Lipsky M., (1980) *Street Level Bureaucracy: Dilemmas of the individual in public services*, Sage, Beverly Hills

Lipsky M., (1989) *The Paradox of Managing Discretionary Workers in Social Welfare Policy*, Paper presented at the Seminar on Sociology of Social Security, University of Edinburgh, July 4th-6th

McEldowney J.J., (1997) 'Policy Evaluation and the Concepts of Deadweight and Additionality: A Commentary', *Evaluation*, Vol.3. No.2, pp.175-188

McGraw S.A. *et al.* (1996) 'Evaluation of the Child and Adolescent Trial for Cardiovascular Health (CATCH)', in *Evaluation and Program Planning*, Vol 19.

Mark T. & Brennan B., (1995) 'Demarketing Health Care', *Journal of Health Services Management*, Vol.4, No.3

Mead L., (1997) *From Welfare to Work: Lessons from America*, IEA Health and Welfare Unit, London

Metcalfe L. & Richards S., (1990) *Improving Public Management*, Sage, London

Montgomery K. & Oliver A. L., (1996) 'Responses by Professional Organisations to Multiple and Ambiguous Institutional Environments: The case of AIDS', *Organization Studies*, Vol. 17, pp.649-671

Morgan G., (1990) *Organisations in Society*, Sage, London

Osborne T., (1997) 'Of Health and Statecraft', in Petersen A., and Brunton R., (eds) *Foucault: Health and medicine*, Routledge, London

Page R., (1995) 'Controlling the Suits: Restoring the Public Service Ethos in the National Health Service', *Association of Clinical Pathologists News*, Autumn

Page R., Silburn B. & Shaw I., (1994) 'Delivering Social Services at a Local Level: Will Reorganisation Matter?', *Public Money and Management*, Vol.14, No.1, Blackwell, Oxford

Parsons, T., (1964) 'Suggestions for a Sociological Approach to The Theory of Organisations', in Etzioni A., (1964) *Complex Organisations: A Sociological Approach*, Rinehart & Winston, New York, pp. 32-38

Parton N., (1994) 'Problematics of Government', *British Journal of Social Work*, Vol.24, pp. 9-32

Patton M.Q., (1980) *Qualitative Evaluation Methods*, Sage, Newbury Park

Patton M.Q., (1986) *Utilization Focussed Evaluation*, Sage, New York

Pawson R., (1996) 'Three Steps to Constructivist Heaven', *Evaluation*, Vol.2, No.2, pp.213-219

Pawson R. & Tilley N., (1997) *Realistic Evaluation*, Sage, London

Pierson C., (1994) *Dismantling the Welfare State? Regan, Thatcher and the politics of retrenchment*, CUP, Cambridge

Pierson C., (1998) *Beyond the Welfare State: The new political economy of welfare*, Polity Press, Cambridge

Pollitt C. & Bouckaert G., (1995) *Quality Improvement in European Public Services*, Sage, London

Powell M. & Hewitt M. (1998) 'The End of the Welfare State?', *Social Policy & Administration*, Vol. 32, No.1

Rawls J., (1985) *Justice as Fairness: Political not metaphysical*, Macmillan, London

Report of the Social Services Committee of the House of Commons, (1988) HMSO, p.xi

Rogers A., Pilgrim D. & Lacy R., (1993) *Experiencing Psychiatry: Users views of services*, Macmillan, London

Roper S., (1993) *Manufacturing Profitability on Northern Ireland*, NIERC, Belfast

Rosenbaum D., (1988) 'Community Crime Prevention: A Review and Synthesis of the Literature', *Justice Quarterly*, Vol.5, pp.325-395

Rutman L., (1984) *Evaluation Research Methods*, Sage, London

Sackett D.L., (1991) *Clinical Epidemiology: A basic science for medicine*, Little Brown, Boston

Samuelson P.A., (1955) *Economics*, McGraw Hill, New York

Scheffler R., (1992) 'Adverse Selection: The Achilles Heel of the NHS Reforms', Lancet 1, pp. 950-952

Scheid T.L. & Greenley J.R., (1997) 'Evaluations of Organizational Effectiveness in Mental Health Programs', *Journal of Health and Social Behaviour*, Vol.38, No.4, pp. 403-427

Scriven M., (1997) *Evaluation Thesaurus* (4th Ed), Sage, Newbury Park, CA

Shaw I., (1994) *Evaluating Interprofessional Training*, Avebury, Aldershot

Shaw I., (1997) 'Evaluation in Health and Social Care: Exploring Lost Dimensions', *Evaluation*, Vol.3, No.4, pp.469-481

Sheard M.H., Martini J.L., Bridges C.L. & Wagner E., (1976) 'The Effect of Lithium on Implusive Aggressive Behaviour in Man', *American Journal of Psychiatry*, Vol.133, No.12, pp.1409-1413

Sheehan M., (1993) 'Government Financial Assistance and Manufacturing Investment in Northern Ireland', *Regional Studies*, Vol.27, pp. 527-540

Silverman D., (1971) *The Theory of Organizations*, Basic Books, New York

Sinclair I. & Goldberg E.M., (1988) *Problems, Tasks and Outcomes: The evaluation of task centered casework in three settings*, Allen & Unwin, London

Sjoberg G., (1975) 'Politics, Ethics and Evaluation Research', in Guttentag M. & Struening E.L., (eds) *Handbook of Evaluation Research* (vol.2) Sage, Beverly Hills, CA

Smith G. & Cantley C., (1995) *Assessing Health Care: A study in organisational evaluation*, Open University Press, Milton Keynes

Strauss A.L., (1978) *Negotiations: Varieties, contexts, processes and social order*, Jossey Bass, San Fransisco

Strong P. & Dingwall R., (1989) 'Romantics and Stoics', in Silverman D. & Gubrium J.F., (eds) *The Politics of Field Research: Sociology beyond enlightenment*, Sage, London

Suchman E., (1967) *Evaluation Research*, Russell Sage, New York

Szasz T.S., (1963) *Law Liberty and Psychiatry*, Macmillan, New York

Talbot R., (1994) *Reinventing Public Management*, Chapman Hall, London

Taylor, B., (1975) *A Management Development and Training Handbook*, Penguin, Harmondsworth

Thompson J.D., (1967) *Organisations in Action*, McGraw Hill, New York

Trosa A., (1994) 'Next Steps: Teaching Giants to Dance', *Social Policy & Administration*, Vol.28, No.2

Vecchio R.P., (1991) *Organisational Behaviour*, Dryden, New York

Weiss C., (1972) *Evaluation Research*, Prentice Hall, Englewood Cliffs NJ

Weiss C., (1990) 'Evaluation for Decisions', in Alkin M. (ed) *Debates on Evaluation*, Sage, Newbury Park, CA

Weiss C., (1996) 'Theory Based Evaluation: Past, Present and Future', paper presented to the American Evaluation Association Conference, Atlanta, Georgia, November 8th

Whalen T., (1977) 'A Crisis in Health', *New York Times*, 26th April

Yuchman E. & Seashore S., (1967) 'A Systems Resource Approach to Organizational Effectiveness', *American Sociological Review*, Vol. 32, pp.891-903

For Product Safety Concerns and Information please contact our EU representative GPSR@taylorandfrancis.com Taylor & Francis Verlag GmbH, Kaufingerstraße 24, 80331 München, Germany

T - #0157 - 270225 - C0 - 219/151/6 - PB - 9781138739581 - Gloss Lamination